WINNING NUMBERS: A DEEP DIVE INTO THE LOTTERY & LUCK

Jeff Copetas

ISBN: 979-8-9892172-0-5
ISBN-13: 979-8-9892172-0-5

For Stephanie, Nathan, Zachary and Dad

Foreward

The Washington Capitals entered the National Hockey League as an expansion team in the 1974–75 season. They proceeded to have the worst individual season in league history, winning 8 games, tying 5...and losing 67. Imagine being a player on that team and having to experience not only the humiliation of losing 90%[1] of the time but having to endure the terrible smell that is hockey equipment. It is safe to say that they didn't get to visit the White House that season.

Move a bit northwest to Ohio where the 1899 Cleveland Spiders baseball team put together a season for the ages, winning 20 games...and losing 134. That is a whole bunch of losing—about 88% of the time they took the field, to be exact. They were so bad that other teams actually refused to travel to Cleveland, forcing the Spiders to play most of their games on the road. Can you imagine that happening today, in the age of major league sports owner's obsessions over ticketing, parking, and concession revenue?

I'd be remiss to not share another fun fact about the 1899 Spiders: player and manager Lave Cross was traded after the

---

[1] https://records.nhl.com/franchises/washington-capitals/season-by-season-record

1

team got off to an 8-30 start. That's right, the manager! Insert skipper Joe Quinn, who led the team to 12 wins…and 104 more losses. Tough summer on the Cuyahoga.

There are a myriad of lovable loser stories weaving their way through history. The Buffalo Bills lost four consecutive Super Bowls from 1991–1994. At least they won enough games to get there. But 30 or so years later, it is still common fodder for sarcastic conversation among football fans and a real pain for the lovely folks on Lake Erie.

Worst of all might be the five NFL teams since 1944[2] that didn't win a single game, not one, in an entire season: the 1960 Dallas Cowboys (0–11–1), the 1976 Tampa Bay Buccaneers (0–14), the 1982 Baltimore Colts in a strike-shortened season (0-8-1), the 2008 Detroit Lions (0–16), and the 2017 Cleveland Browns (0–16).

What is it with Cleveland and losing, by the way?

It leads me to ask the question *who are the very best losers of all time?* Over the years, who has lost and lost and lost yet kept trying and trying and trying? What could be worse than an NFL team having sixteen 50/50 chances to win only to come up short every time? Who's at the very bottom of the barrel?

I spent hours digging through sports statistics and other woeful tales of losing. Here's some more:

- In the early 1960s, Dick Rowe was a music executive for London's Decca Records. His job: find new bands and sell more records. One particular day in 1962 there were two bands auditioning at the Decca studios. One band, The Tremeloes, was signed to Decca. Upon hearing the other band, Rowe told the

---

[2] https://americanfootball.fandom.com/wiki/Imperfect_season

band's manager that "guitar groups are on the way out." That second band? The Beatles. Oops.[3]

- Nelson, William, and Lamar Hunt were already fabulously wealthy when Nelson, fearing U.S. government interference with their vast wealth, convinced his brothers to buy a boatload of silver - almost 7 million pounds, nearly half of the world's silver. March 27th, 1980 became known as "Silver Thursday" - prices collapsed and brothers lost over a billion dollars. Nelson Hunt broke the record for the biggest personal bankruptcy in US history.[4]
- How can I not mention Sam Bankman-Fried? With the November 2022 collapse of FTX (a crypto exchange), he lost a staggering $23 billion dollars in just three weeks and remains under investigation globally for possible securities violations.[5]

I found so many losers, I began feeling bad for the whole world. Then I found it! I found the biggest losers of them all. It's me. I'm the loser. And you. You're a loser. And pretty much everyone you know. We are all losers.

When it comes to state and national lotteries in the U.S.A., the losing is stunning, sad, and mystifying. And it needs to be explained. Perhaps in a book. This book. And if you are one of the very very very very very rare winners, that too is stunning. Also sometimes sad and mystifying.

This book follows the lives of a few of those lottery winners, including first-hand accounts of what their lives

---

[3] https://historycollection.com/biggest-losers-in-history/

[4] https://historycollection.com/biggest-losers-in-history

[5] https://www.forbes.com/sites/darreonnadavis/2023/06/02/what-happened-to-ftx-the-crypto-exchange-funds-collapse-explained/?sh=1c1db943cb7b

were like before they won, their reactions and mindsets on the day they won, and the details of their lives after winning. Some have adeptly turned their winnings into a sweet, comfortable life and others, well, they have not.

This book will also explore a short history of lotteries, rife with celebration, controversy, organized crime, and unbelievable tales of woe. I will detail the different and insane odds of winning a jackpot. By reading this book, you'll know more about the lives of the lawyers and law firms who operate trusts for anonymous winners. You'll learn from an arguably obsessed consumer watchdog of lotteries in Texas, the head of the state lottery commission in Arizona, and the Executive Director of the National Council on Problem Gambling. And since the lottery is a numbers game, there's a fair amount of numerical statistics coming at you that will walk through the odds, explain who plays the lottery, and offer some sobering metrics around gambling addiction. You'll even meet a person who makes a living by losing on scratch tickets.

One of the winners I spoke with wished to remain anonymous. This was a very common theme, and, more often than not, a complete deal-breaker with many refusing to even speak with me about their experiences. Because of this wish to remain anonymous, I have changed the aforementioned winner's name to protect their identity, which provided them comfort in telling the details of their story. In the end, it's less about who they are specifically and more about providing you, the reader, with details about what happens when you actually win.

Which you won't.

By the end of this book, you and I will still be consistent losers.

Maybe playing for the Capitals, Spiders, Bills, and all those other losing teams wasn't so bad. After all, those players had the benefit of camaraderie, of shared joy, luxuriating in the aroma of the post-game locker room. They likely have some entertaining stories to match the gift of lifelong friendships. And let's not forget, they got paid to lose. Not us, though. We PAY to lose.

I'll take 10 quick picks, please.

CHAPTER ONE

Games People Play

Lotteries, while not born in the U.S.A., have existed in this country since the 17th century. And while the name Ainsworth Rand Spofford may invoke the image of an Ivy League lacrosse player, alas, that is not the case here. Spofford was the sixth Librarian of Congress, and he served 10 U.S. presidents from 1864 to 1897.[6] During his tenure, he combed through periodicals and newspapers as part of an exercise to find the earliest lottery notifications ever published. In the American Weekly Mercury, he found a notice of a lottery occurring in February 1720[7]. It may not have been the first, but it is the earliest lottery Spofford found in a publication. The lucky jackpot winner was to receive a brick house on the corner of Third and Arch in Philadelphia, Pennsylvania. Tickets were 20 shillings each and sales were capped at 350 tickets. Players had much better odds at winning that house

---

[6] https://www.loc.gov/item/n90613873/ainsworth-rand-spofford-1825-1908/

[7] https://www.atlasobscura.com/articles/early-american-lottery-ticket-colonial

than of being struck by lightning.

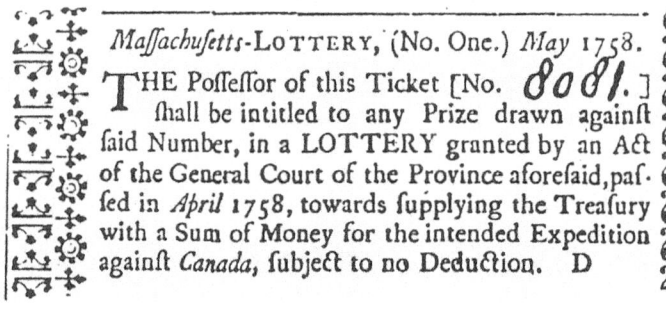

A ticket for a lottery in Massachusetts, 1758. RON SHELLEY/PUBLIC DOMAIN

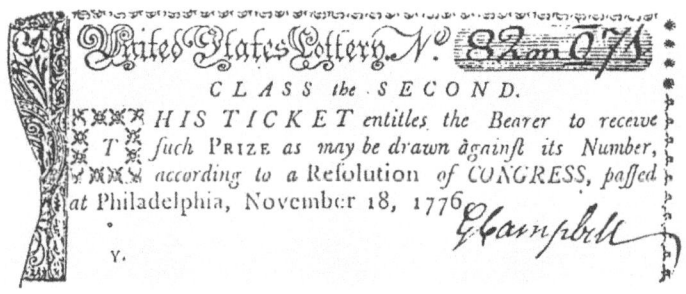

The Continental Congress used lotteries to raise money, 1776. RON SHELLEY/PUBLIC DOMAIN

Images courtesy of Atlas Obscura[8]

Outside of the U.S.A., there is evidence that the first lottery tickets to award money were held in the 15th century in the "Low Countries," what we know today as the Netherlands[9].

---

[8] https://www.atlasobscura.com/articles/early-american-lottery-ticket-colonial

[9] R. Shelley (1989). The Lottery Encyclopedia. Austin, TX: Byron Pub. Services. p. 109

One scholar reports a cash prize lottery held in Florence, Italy as early as 1530. From there, other nearby countries picked up using lotteries, largely for the purpose of fundraising. The British crown came around to the notion of lotteries in 1569 and by the time the 1700s rolled around, raising money through lotteries was viewed more as a resourceful way to generate money for public projects and public good as opposed to the frenetic public cash grab its known for today. The early 1700s found the Archbishop of Canterbury tying his name to lotteries[10] for the purpose of funding the British Museum and Westminster Bridge.

The first recorded lottery in the American colonies was organized by the Virginia Company of London in 1612 as a one-time event to raise funds for the struggling settlement of what is now Jamestown, Virginia.

"As pitched by the Virginia Company, buying a lottery ticket was an act of charity that could save a savage's soul," Matthew Sweeney writes in *The Lottery Wars*.[11]

There were not enough convenience stores, gas stations, or grocery stores to support an ongoing lottery operation to save all of the souls of Virginians. It would take another 375 years before this singular event would become today's Virginia Lottery.

According to the North American Association of State and Provincial Lotteries (NAPSL), the first modern lottery occurred in the state of New Hampshire and was called the

---

[10] https://www.atlasobscura.com/articles/early-american-lottery-ticket-colonial

[11] https://books.google.com/books?id=MEqgAwAAQBAJ&pg=PP5&lpg=PP5&dq=The+Lottery+Wars:+Long+Odds,+Fast+Money,+and+the+Battle+Over+an+American+Institution

New Hampshire Sweepstakes[12]. Not based on picking numbers, but on picking horses, the first lottery tickets for it were sold on March 12, 1964.[13] It didn't take long for other states to realize that lotteries were a great way to drive revenue for the state without angering its residents with tax increases. This was an important realization, as it set the stage for lottery-related hyper-growth for all states in the coming decades and years.

The 1970s saw a major shift with the introduction of the first multi-state lotteries. And once state governments and lottery administrators recognized the large source of cash revenue from these games, perspectives changed and more lotteries were introduced. These multi-state lotteries, essential precursors to what we know today as games like Powerball and Mega Millions, offered larger jackpots and became very popular with players. While the amounts we know today—of jackpots in the hundreds of millions and even billions weren't comprehendible yet, the '70s did mark the beginning of a gold rush of sorts: Americans were more willing to risk more money on lotteries as jackpot amounts increased.

Then, in the 1980s, the United States lottery industry experienced significant growth and evolution, with scratch tickets generating large interest. Things were moving quickly now, and the Multi-State Lottery Association (MUSL) was formed in 1987[14] to put formality behind multi-state lotteries. With that, the first real modern-day multi-state jackpot game, called Lotto America (known today as Powerball), was born. With all of this came an increased presence of lottery advertising. While the promise of huge gobs of cash prizes

---

[12] https://www.naspl.org/historyofthelottery

[13] https://www.naspl.org/historyofthelottery

[14] https://www.lottoamerica.com/musl

didn't really require much advertising, the campaigns sought to sing the benefits of state revenue, such as increased funding for education initiatives.

If the '80s saw Porsche-like acceleration in terms of accessibility and mass exposure, the 1990s was the Lamborghini—we can't take the time to argue about which maker is better right now. In the span of just these ten years, lottery revenue grew by $5 billion as more and more states jumped into the pool. Now cognizant of the gigantic revenue streams, late stragglers like Colorado and Kentucky moved to establish state lottery systems as well. Through it all, states were still advertising their altruistic uses of lottery revenue (so virtuous!). But the race was on, and advertising began to incorporate more promises of instant wealth. Hence, the Lamborghini. By the end of the 90s, a person could walk into a convenience store and go into choice overload just looking at the large amount of scratch ticket options. The price of scratch tickets started to creep up, with higher-priced tickets offering a bigger prize. Perhaps the largest change in lotteries during the 1990s, though, was the emergence of the modern-day heavy hitters, Mega Millions and Powerball.

Entering the 2000s, U.S. citizens were spending more on lottery games and prize amounts were growing. The train kept a-rollin' as it seemed every year brought a new "wow" moment for Powerball and Mega Millions as jackpot records were regularly eclipsed.

As seems to always be the case, this increased revenue brought with it new kinds of corruption and finger-pointing. Enter more reform! In 2002, the Bipartisan Campaign Reform Act, known to most people today as the McCain-Feingold Act, banned the use of lottery proceeds for political campaign advertising. This new law completely ended the suspicious funding of election campaigns forever and ever.

Oh wait, no it didn't. "Dark money[15]" still infiltrates political campaigns. But I digress…

In 2010—to the surprise of exactly nobody—the first online lottery sales began in the state of Illinois, and the first mobile app was launched with lottery functionality. People could now purchase lottery tickets and see their winnings on an app instead of going to the grocery store, gas station, or convenience store. Easy, fast, and addictive. America!

With inflation now being a hot-button topic and the volume of jackpot amounts getting into the billions with more frequency, LendingTree wanted to know more about who purchases tickets and how much each purchaser spends. In their 2022 study[16] on lottery habits in 2020, they looked at how much money people spend on lotteries by state. Then they examined the data from the lens of income and affordability. They also surveyed approximately 2,000 U.S.-based consumers about their approach and habits when it comes to lotteries.

The study found that Massachusetts residents spent the most per capita on the lottery (scratch tickets and numbers games) at $805.30 per capita in 2020. And it wasn't a close race. New York ($455.93) and Rhode Island ($429.88) were second and third on the list, but look at those deltas—the residents of Massachusetts spent almost double the second-place state. At the bottom end of the study's list we find that the people of North Dakota spent $32.24 per capita, below Wyoming ($40.97) and Montana ($58.62). What does this say about the residents of Massachusetts? Or North Dakota, for

---

[15] https://www.theguardian.com/commentisfree/2022/aug/29/billions-in-dark-money-is-influencing-us-politics-we-need-disclosure-laws

[16] https://www.lendingtree.com/debt-consolidation/lottery-study/

that matter?

Perhaps part of the reason is that in terms of average return, Massachusetts residents got back 70 cents in lottery prize money for every dollar they spent in 2020. Only Missourians saw a better return at 71 cents per dollar. At first glance, 70 cents back for every dollar spent in a game of chance with very low odds doesn't seem terrible until you break out the math over huge swaths of cash outlays. Looking at 2021 metrics per the North American Association of State and Provincial Lotteries (NASPL), Massachusetts residents spent $5.8 billion and won back $4.2 billion of that. The Massachusetts State Lottery Association banked a cool $1.6 billion off its residents in 2021.

That same year in South Dakota, players won back only 19 cents per dollar. West Virginia (22 cents) and Oregon (23 cents) were nearly as low.

A separate but equally interesting LendingTree research survey showed 86% of lottery players buy scratch tickets, 65% buy Powerball-style number-drawing tickets, and 58% of players said they'd take an upfront, lump-sum payment if they win the big one.[17] There's some interesting math later on the "upfront" vs "annuity" question.

Before that, let's take a look at some of the biggest and most well-known lottery games in the United States.

POWERBALL

The concept is pretty simple. Players first pick five numbers ranging from 1 to 69. Then they pick one Powerball number; any number from 1 to 26. If the player matches all five main numbers and the Powerball, they win big!

The first drawing was held in 1988 and was known as Lotto America. After four short years, the powers that be

---

[17] https://www.lendingtree.com/debt-consolidation/lottery-study/

were so bored from counting all the money that they decided to change the name to Powerball. The first drawing under the re-branded name was held on April 22, 1992 in West Des Moines, Iowa and, for the next 29 years, the winning balls were drawn each Wednesday and Saturday night.

Starting in 2012, Powerball took its talents south (another sneaky Cleveland reference), and today the winning balls are yanked out of barrels at the Florida Lottery's studio in Tallahassee. The minimum amount of winnings for each jackpot is $20 million USD and a second prize of $1 million can be won. That can go up to $2 million if the player bets more via the Power Play option. The game was huge and becoming huger (my editor says huger is not a word, but I like it).

It doesn't take a business genius to see that many, many players were frothing for more opportunities to lose. The smart business people at Powerball headquarters were very aware that they could just keep take-take-taking the money, so they happily did. Eventually realizing they could take more, a third weekly drawing was added in August 2021. Now, drawings are held on Monday, Wednesday and Saturday.

Today, the Powerball is available in 45 U.S. states, plus the District of Columbia, Puerto Rico, and the U.S. Virgin Islands. It is coordinated by the Multi-State Lottery Association (MUSL), which, according to its website[18], is "a non-profit association that assists its member lotteries in multi-jurisdictional game development. Each MUSL member offers one or more of the games generally facilitated by MUSL, but retains its independent statutory duties regarding ticket sales, retailer authorization, prize payments, income offsets, and other responsibilities." Aside from that mouthful, their

---

[18] https://www.musl.com/index.html

website offers little-to-no more detail about the organization and looks as if it's designed and maintained by a sophomore in high school who just learned that moving titles aren't cool. That said, 38 U.S. state lotteries are members of MUSL and the organization has serious power behind it.

MEGA MILLIONS

Originally called The Big Game, what is known today as Mega Millions kicked off with a weekly drawing held each Friday. Six U.S. states participated in the first 1996 drawing: Virginia, Massachusetts, Illinois, Georgia, Maryland and Michigan. It took fewer than two years for a second weekly drawing to be added on Tuesdays. A year later, New Jersey jumped onto the list of participating states.

Much like Powerball, Mega Millions' players pick a total of six numbers from two distinct pools. The first pick is to choose five numbers from the pool of 1 to 70 and the second pick is to choose a single number from the pool 1 to 25. This second pick is the Mega Ball and if you used your magical powers of random-number picking and hit all six numbers, the only payout option was an annual payout over multiple years.

In January 1999, that changed. The Big Game added a cash-upfront option for jackpot winners and also expanded the pool of numbers in the drawing. By May 2002, the name was changed to Mega Millions and two more states were added to the mix, Ohio and New York, making the game available in nine U.S. states. Over the next eight years, 26 more states were added to the list, making Mega Millions the most-played lottery game in the U.S., available in 35 states and seeing an explosive volume of losers. Today, Mega Millions is offered in 45 U.S. states and 2 jurisdictions (the District of Columbia and the U.S. Virgin Islands).

* * *

There are a few major differences between Mega Millions and Powerball.

Mega Millions jackpots start at $40 million with a second prize going as high as $5 million via the optional Megaplier, which requires—surprise—additional investment from the player.

The final difference, and the reason why the odds of winning Mega Millions are slightly tougher than Powerball, is that Mega Millions numbers are from 1 to 70 whereas Powerball is from 1 to 69. The Mega Ball also ranges from 1 to 25, whereas in Powerball it's 1 to 26. Adding this one number may not seem like a lot, but the math is solid. Trust me.

Until 2010, retailers could only offer one or the other; Powerball or Mega Millions. But January 31, 2010 brought a watershed moment in these high-jackpot multi-state lotteries —MUSL and the Mega Millions consortium aligned and agreed to offer cross-selling of both games, meaning people could now walk into any store and play both games. It is unlikely that the satisfaction and happiness of customers was the primary reason. Is it ever? In an article[19] posted on CNN when the deal was struck in October 2009, CNNMoney.com staff writer Aaron Smith wrote:

> "Millions of lottery players will be able to double their bets because of a deal announced Wednesday by the two powerhouses of the business. Mega Millions and Powerball, the country's largest lotteries, will allow stores in many states to sell both lotteries. The agreement 'means that lotteries from across the United States, and the U.S. Virgin Islands, will be able to choose to offer their lottery players both jackpot

---

[19] https://money.cnn.com/2009/10/14/news/companies/powerball_mega_millions/index.htm

games via their retailers,' Mega Millions said in a statement."

Key takeaway: "double their bets." Hmm. A nice way to say "lose more money."

The Winnings

Jackpot winners for Powerball and Mega Millions now have two options to collect their newfound riches; they can take a huge wheelbarrow of cash upfront, or be paid annually in installments over a longer time period. OK, it's not actually a wheelbarrow, but it's fun to imagine a winner demanding that exact method of cash delivery. Now I will let my mind wander over the different ways a person could receive that amount of money while you continue reading.

Each option has benefits and drawbacks. The cash-upfront option means the winner gets less money, but offers a significant amount of cash upfront to spend or invest immediately. Many winners appear to choose this option. Opting for the annual payments over 30 years allows the winner to collect far more money in the long run, but have less cash upfront. And let's not forget taxes…

Let's use the Powerball jackpot of $215 million from December 27, 2022, to break down the two options.

The Cash Option:

If the winner elects to take the cash-upfront option, the winning amount is determined by the number of tickets sold for that time period plus any prior time period where there were no jackpot winners. The entity that runs Powerball needs to have the total amount of the cash option on hand to pay out to the winner immediately. In this case, Powerball estimated that $112.3 million worth of tickets had been sold since the last time someone won a jackpot. Our winner is already down to $112.3 million in winnings out of the advertised jackpot of $215 million. That is before Uncle Sam even comes knocking. Take the standard federal tax deduction of 24%, which hacks another $26.9 million from the winnings. Our winner is now down to $85.4 million. Don't think for a second that tax responsibilities stop there—our lucky winner is now in the top tax bracket in the U.S. (37%) due to their wheelbarrow of upfront cash, so come tax time in April, whack another 13% off the winnings (24% + 13% = 37%). Cough up another $14.5 million. At this point, the winner now has $70 million. The tax reaper still isn't finished, though.

It's at this point where the next set of taxes becomes variable depending on the state the winner resides in. The best places to live for lottery winners are Florida, Texas, Wyoming, Washington state, Tennessee, Alaska, New Hampshire, South Dakota, and Nevada because they don't have state income taxes. California is excellent as well, as lottery winnings are exempt from state taxes. Other great places for a winner to live are Ohio (from 0% to 3.99%) or North Dakota (from 1.1% to 2.9%). Eyeballing the list of state taxes on the handy USAMega website[20] (and assuming a married filing jointly tax submission), it would appear the average state tax is 5%. Assuming that average rate of 5%, chop off another $5.6 million. Finally, our winner can breathe. Picking the cash option nets $65 million out of a $215 million jackpot.

But you don't need to feel bad for our winner (even though the winnings are ~$150 million less than advertised). If the winner just plops that $65 million into a regular savings account generating 1% annual interest, they would be a)

---

[20] https://www.usamega.com/powerball/jackpot/2022/12/28/married-filing-jointly

dumb and b) easily living off interest alone, which would be about $650,000 in year one and go up from there due to compounding interest. Either way, it's still very much time to party down.

The Annual Payment Option:

If our winner is playing for the long haul, the annual payment option will net them significantly more money, but they have to wait a really long time to realize it; 30 years to be exact. In our $215 million jackpot scenario, the full amount is awarded. How? Because the Powerball brass will take the value of the upfront cash option and invest it so that the winner will receive the full amount over the course of 30 years as an annuity. The value of each subsequent payment after year one increases each year until all 30 payments are deposited. As with the upfront option, taxes also apply here. The gross prize of $215 million divided by 30 years is $7.1 million dollars per year. Once again, subtract the 24% Federal tax rate ($1.7m) to help pay for the U.S.A.'s Military Industrial Complex (pure conjecture), add another 13% in April to get you to the highest tax bracket ($866k), and then add the average 5% state tax ($358k). Our winner brings home about $4.2 million in year one and they end up with a total of $126 million over 30 years. Once again, party time.

Let's summarize this in a neat table. Assuming that one person wins the $215 million jackpot amount that was up for grabs on December 27, 2022, here are the Cliff Notes on both payout options with the breakdown:

	Annual Payment	Cash Upfront
Total Jackpot	$215,000,000	$112,300,000
Gross winnings	$7,166,667/year	$112,300,000
Federal Tax (24%)	-$1,720,000/year	-$26,952,000
More Federal Tax (13%)	-$866,216/year	-$14,533,549
Avg. State Tax (5%)	-$358,333/year	-$5,615,000
Net Winnings	$4,222,118/year	$65,199,141
Total Winnings	$126,663,540 (30 years)	$65,199,141

The total winnings for the annual payment option exceeds the cash-upfront option by $61 million dollars. If our winner is willing to wait 30 years. However, if the winner takes all that cash upfront and saves or invests it wisely, it's quite possible that the wheelbarrow of upfront money could exceed that $126 million 30 years down the road.

So what's the better option? Cash upfront or annuity? Well, like most things, it's complicated. Jay Zagorsky is a Professor of Markets, Public Policy, and Law at Boston University's Questrom School of Business. He has spent over two decades researching a wide variety of personal wealth topics, performing many studies about inheritances. This guy knows a lot about wealth! In my conversation with him, he offered this advice:

"I say if you win a lottery, always always take the annual payout," he says confidently. Why? "Because nobody is prepared for a huge windfall like that. I'd say get those first one or two payouts and then you'll figure out how to actually run your life."

Zagorsky adds that the people in favor of taking the upfront cash always cite the benefit of being able to invest more of it at the start, but the Professor contends that it takes a long, long time to learn how to invest $500 million. You don't just take a check to the local bank and drop it in your savings account. And yes, you'll have enough money to build a team to help you, but they won't necessarily instill spending discipline into your new life.

"So my standard advice is always to take the annual payout," Zagorsky says, then he adds, "That said, I don't think there has been a single big lottery winner for a very long time that's taken the annuity."

But maybe more people should.

Winning the lottery isn't likely to change a person's historical approach to spending, which could make an upfront cash sum very dangerous for a reckless spender. This makes Zagorsky's advice pretty sound. Take the annual payment to give yourself time to adjust. It may not be the best option financially, but take it from a guy who has taught finance at renowned business schools for 20-plus years. Jay contends that it's not always about earning the absolute maximum amount of return; it's about your discipline and what you've saved. He then explains "the rule of 70" to drive home the point.

"The rule of 70 asks how long it takes something to double in size. If you're earning 7% interest, then 70 divided by seven means that every ten years, the amount will double." He went on to explain that people argue it is better to take the lump-sum payout and invest it all in the stock markets, capitalizing on the rule of 70.

"But my standard response to most people who've asked me that is to just ask them if they can imagine spending $500 million," he says. "And they're like, no."

But not everyone agrees with Zagorsky's advice.

Kurt Panouses is a Florida-based lawyer who handles many big-money lottery clients. You will hear much more from him later in these pages, but his approach is to almost always take the lump sum. He explains, "Most clients want the lump sum payment to begin with. Generally, I like to see them in control of their money and most financial advisors believe they can outperform the rate of return offered by the state with the annuity." He went on to explain that states cannot invest in anything that isn't safe. By statute, they are limited to and typically invest in lower-risk treasuries. Panouses did say that on the rare occasion that he works with a 20 or 30-year-old winner, his advice may change. Younger winners "may want to consider the annuity as they may not be able to control their spending habits. I did have a retired teacher take the payments because if she lived more than 20 years, it would be better income tax-wise."

Ultimately, his advice is to take the lump sum. "If you take the annuity, you have to go through the payout process 29 additional times, so there's a better chance for there to be a leak of who won," Panouses concludes.

So what happens if a jackpot winner opts for the Annual Payment option and dies within the 30-year period? The following statement appears on Powerball's website:

> *"If a jackpot winner dies before receiving all annual installments, the balance of the prize will be paid to the winner's estate. Upon receipt of a court order, annual prize payments will continue to be paid to the winner's heirs. Other provisions may also apply depending on the laws of the lottery paying the prize."*

But what if the winner didn't set up a trust or an estate? Panouses has this to say: "If you die, almost every state I know of pays it outright in a lump sum to a beneficiary. All states are different, though."

SCRATCH TICKETS

These probably need very little explanation. In the big picture, scratch tickets are a newer form of the lottery, making their first appearance in the U.S.A. in 1974. The first state to offer them was…New Hampshire. Again! The "Live Free or Die" state was ahead of its time in giving residents an exciting offering that almost guaranteed losing money.

Scratch tickets also seem to have built up a befuddling amount of different names over the years, if Wikipedia[21] is to be believed. The Wikipedia article on scratch tickets says, "A scratchcard (also called a scratch off, scratch ticket, scratcher, scratchum, scratch-it, scratch game, scratch-and-win, instant game, instant lottery, scratchie, lot scrots, or scritchies) is a card designed for competitions, often made of thin cardstock or plastic to conceal PINs, where one or more areas contain concealed information, revealed by scratching off an opaque covering." Hands up if you've ever heard of a "scratchum," a "lot scrot" or a "scritchie".

Because they are generally cheap, scratch tickets are an extremely popular form of gambling here in the United States. It's not just the low cost, either. They appear to be available for purchase everywhere, especially where people make quick stops: convenience stores, grocery stores, or gas stations. They are cheap, easy to buy and, oh yeah, a majority provide a winning or losing result instantaneously, meaning people don't have to wait for numbers to be drawn on a specific night. And U.S. players show up in droves to buy them. Look no further than the Reddit lottery board[22], which boasts 26,600 members as of February 2023, and generates a boatload of activity on a daily basis. Almost every post by this Reddit community details the results of their scratch ticket investment. If an alien landed on Earth with a full

---

[21] https://en.wikipedia.org/wiki/Scratchcard
[22] https://www.reddit.com/r/Lottery/

comprehension of all things financial, they would wonder how people could be so entranced by such a losing proposition.

One of the more interesting trends seen on the Reddit board is the people who purchase scratch tickets in *books* or *rolls*. Both terms are interchangeable, so for now we'll stick with the term *book*. This means, effectively, purchasing tickets in bulk in order to increase the chance of winning, as each book does guarantee a certain number of winning tickets. The number of tickets in a book really depends on the price of a single ticket. Since scratch ticket prices are typically priced at $2, $5, $10, $20 or $50, the price of a book can vary. To make this easier, most books have a standardized price of $300, so if you buy a $2 book, you get 150 tickets, and so on.

Many people on the Reddit lottery board post the results of their purchase of scratch ticket books, and it's fascinating, to say the least. For example, there are multiple posts that detail people getting a $200 return on a $300 investment, and then using that $200 to buy more lottery tickets, putting them deeper in the hole. It's mystifying. While there are occasional winning tickets posted, the Reddit board is not a place to be if you're confident that you'll come out ahead in any scratch ticket scenario.

We'll hear more from one of the frequent contributors to the Reddit board in a later chapter.

Another interesting trend with scratch tickets is that, similar to Powerball and Mega Millions, some of the larger prizes allow a winner to choose an upfront payout or an annuity. Not all tickets offer this and some winning tickets are only paid out annually. So even scratch tickets are starting to creep away from the notion of instant winning.

A quick aside: Most people's minds go straight to lottery tickets when the topic of scratch cards comes up, but there is one non-lottery instance that is worth mentioning as an interesting side note. During the 1980–1981 NHL hockey season, the most predominant sports trading card company at the time, Topps, released their card set for the season. Each card had the names of the players obscured and no names on the back of the card, either. Card owners would have to scratch off a puck-shaped area on the card to reveal who the player was. As one might imagine, these were not popular with hardcore collectors, who were unhappy at having to potentially damage a card with a coin. As it turns out, the collectors smartly left them unscratched - and those are worth more today than the scratched ones.

* * *

Aside from wondering how it was even possible that Wayne Gretzky was ever only a *2ⁿᵈ Team All-Star*, your humble author, ten years old at the time, very much enjoyed this card set despite sometimes scratching cards with excessive vigor, destroying the player's name in the process. Internet forms aplenty also indicate this a common experience for others. The fact that these cards still come up in conversation, however, supports the notion that there is no such thing as bad press.

KENO

Keno is a popular numbers game that has a long and rich history and dates back thousands of years to ancient China. The game is thought to have originated during the Han Dynasty, around 205 B.C.E. According to legend, the game was invented by a man named Cheung Leung, who was a prince in ancient China. He came up with the game as a way to raise funds for his army, as his kingdom was facing a financial crisis. The game was a success and soon became popular throughout China and other parts of Asia.

In the United States, Keno was first played in the mid-19th century, initially by Chinese immigrants and later by other groups of settlers. It was often played in bars and taverns and was a popular form of entertainment for miners during the California Gold Rush. In the early 20th century, Keno became a more organized and regulated form of gambling, with standardized rules and a centralized system for drawing numbers. Today, it is a popular casino game, played in various forms around the world.

In Keno, players place a bet by choosing from numbers ranging (in most cases) from 1 through 80. Typically, after all players make their wagers in a given time period, 20 numbers are drawn at random with a ball machine (similar to

Powerball or Bingo), or some kind of online number generator. A player who wins is paid based on how many of their numbers match the drawn numbers.

Surprise! Wins don't happen nearly as often as losses.

DAILY NUMBERS GAMES

Daily numbers games are types of lottery or betting games that involve selecting a set of numbers, usually from a predetermined range, and then waiting for a random drawing to determine the winning numbers. These games are typically played every day, the big hint there being that they are called the "daily numbers game."

One popular example of a daily numbers game in the United States is the common Pick 3 or Pick 4 game. Many states have different marketing names for these games, but the Pick 3 or Pick 4 is the most common methodology. In this game, players choose three or four numbers from 0 to 9, and then a daily drawing takes place and the winning numbers are revealed. The payouts for winning numbers are typically determined by the odds.

Now that you have the basics and understand the major games, let's dig a little deeper into lottery spending in the USA for 2022, using NAPSL's end-of-year summary[23] from its year-end issue of Insights Magazine.

- American lotteries generated $98 billion in sales for traditional lottery games in 2022, largely flat compared to the $98.1 generated in 2021
- Add the $9.9 billion generated from casino games and sports betting, and the 2022 total is $107.9 billion, up 2.5% from 2021

---

[23] https://nasplmatrix.org/insights#insightsViewer/87

- Lotteries turned a net profit of $28.6 billion in fiscal 2022, an increase from $28.2 billion the previous year —this is money for beneficiaries as designated by each state lottery commission
- The top four state lotteries in 2022 were Florida, California, Texas, and New York
- Florida generated the most in 2022 lottery sales, generating $9.3 billion
- Instant games (scratch tickets, mostly) make up two-thirds of traditional game sales in the U.S., generating $64.9 billion

Here's the complete 2022 breakdown from Insights Magazine:

United States Sales Summary

	FY21	FY22	Increase (Decrease)	Percent Ch
Instants	$65,357.0	$64,975.4	($381.6)	
Pull tabs	287.5	316.2	28.7	
Lottery einstants (net)	614.8	644.5	29.8	
Powerball	4,009.5	5,181.5	1,172.0	2
Mega Millions	4,182.7	3,108.8	(1,072.9)	-2
Lotto America	56.7	62.2	5.5	
For Life games *	605.3	693.2	87.9	1
All other lotto games	3,750.0	3,566.7	(183.3)	
Daily numbers (2-5 digits)	13,143.4	12,663.1	(480.2)	
Mon for games	4,906.7	5,351.3	444.8	
Daily keno	67.1	67.6	0.5	
Terminal-based instant games	937.1	1,111.0	173.9	
Raffles	42.5	48.2	5.7	
Hybrid instant/draw games	19.5	13.6	(4.9)	-2
All other games	227.2	329.8	102.8	4
Total draw games	31,946.8	32,138.3	251.4	
Total traditional games	**98,106.1**	**98,034.5**	**(71.6)**	
Electronic gaming machines (net)	6,052.1	8,305.2	2,253.1	3
Table games (net)	79.8	902.7	170.8	
Sports betting (net)	293.2	617.7	324.4	11
Grand total sales	**$105,243.4**	**$107,920.0**	**$2,676.6**	

To sum it up, United States citizens spend gobs and gobs of money trying to win gobs and gobs of even more money, all resulting in people losing gobs and gobs of money. Because money makes everything better. Please repeat that sentence now with a sarcastic tone.

CHAPTER TWO

The Odds

Lottery odds are a funny thing. Say the word lottery and most people's minds go directly to the whoppers—the $250 million prize or even the unthinkable $1 billion-plus bounty, more common in the 2020s. While those are the prizes that get all the TV coverage, an overwhelming amount of lottery spending and winnings happen on the smaller scales, where the scratch tickets are.

These are the lotteries with a higher volume of winners and, if you're reading this book, you've likely experienced those wins more than a few times. They are mildly intoxicating. In a warped kind of way, the term loss-leader applies here as these prizes are the little pittances that keep you coming back for more. Oh, the dreams of winning just a little more. Next time. Always next time…

Take, for example, where you pick your initial five numbers and the magical Powerball number. That single sixth Powerball number is found between the parenthesis on the Powerball slip and you can win a small prize by matching just that single number. The general sentiment is that the odds of matching that single Powerball number to win a prize are 1 in 26, right? Seems simple. Not so. The real odds of matching the singular Powerball are actually more difficult than 1 in 26 because there are 5 more numbers on the card which qualify players to win another prize.

To be more specific and arguably more nerdy, Powerball numbers are picked from two sets of numbers, or barrels if you watch the drawing live. The first barrel contains the initial 69 numbers and the second barrel holds the 26 Powerballs, so the odds of winning the jackpot need to be calculated by a combination of the odds for both. To calculate the odds of hitting the single Powerball number (which awards a prize of $4), you need to pull from two sets of numbers: the odds of matching the single Powerball number from 1 to 26 in one barrel and the odds of not matching any of the five numbers from the numbers picked from the other. The odds of picking only the Powerball, therefore, are not 1-in-26, but 1-in-38.

What about the big stuff, though? It seems that the odds of winning the top prize in a jackpot like Powerball involves strange and random weather incidents: tornadoes, tidal waves, and everyone's favorite, the 'ol lightning strike. Let's explore that last one for a moment.

In 2019, The National Weather Service[24] estimated that the population of the United States was 330,000,000. Aside from trying to remember when or why the National Weather Service last called you for census-taking, they also reported that 27 people were killed and 243 people were injured by lightning strikes, making the odds of being struck by lightning 1 in 1,222,000 million. The closest equivalent to those odds for winning at Powerball would be the $50,000 prize. (You actually have a better chance at winning the $50,000 prize than being hit by lightning, this is just the

---

[24] https://www.weather.gov/safety/lightning-odds

closest comparison to be made.)

The odds of winning the whopper—the Powerball jackpot —are 1 in 292,200,000 million.[25] Gulp.

Here are the odds for Powerball, right from the horse's mouth, the Powerball website:

Match	Prize (USD)	Odds
5 Balls + Powerball	Grand Prize (variable)	1 in 292,201,338
5 Balls, no Powerball	$1,000,000	1 in 11,688,053
4 Balls + Powerball	$50,000	1 in 913,129
4 Balls, no Powerball	$100	1 in 36,525
3 Balls + Powerball	$100	1 in 14,494
3 Balls, no Powerball	$7	1 in 579
2 Balls + Powerball	$7	1 in 701
1 Ball + Powerball	$4	1 in 91
Only Powerball	$4	1 in 38

---

[25] https://www.powerball.com/about

And here are the odds for Mega Millions, from the Mega Millions website:

Match	Prize (USD)	Odds
5 Balls + Mega Ball	Grand Prize (variable)	1 in 302,575,350
5 Balls, no Mega Ball	$1,000,000	1 in 12,607,306
4 Balls + Mega Ball	$10,000	1 in 931,001
4 Balls, no Mega Ball	$500	1 in 38,792
3 Balls + Mega Ball	$200	1 in 14,547
3 Balls, no Mega Ball	$10	1 in 606
2 Balls + Mega Ball	$10	1 in 693
1 Ball + Mega Ball	$4	1 in 89
Only Mega Ball	$2	1 in 37

So while you are more likely to be struck by lightning (not as fun as winning the lottery), an argument can be made that lightning isn't the best way to really envision the odds. Perhaps the better way to compare these odds would be to put yourself somewhere familiar with a whole lot of other people—a football stadium, for example. You can picture this because you've likely been in a stadium before.

Let's say you have Taylor Swift tickets, which had its very own disastrous lottery situation in 2022. Pretend you worked your magic on TicketMaster and you're going to see TSwift perform at Bryant-Denny Stadium in Tuscaloosa, Alabama. This stadium has a capacity of 100,000 people (ok, it's actually

100,077, but let's just pretend that it's exactly 100,000, because…easy math).

Now imagine that the concert is raffling off the chance to meet Taylor Swift after the show, and only one person out of the 100,000 attendees is going to win. How do you feel about your odds?

Now let's go ahead and add 2,922 more sold-out Bryant-Denny stadiums, each full of 100,000 people. And still, only one person will win. Feeling any better? You shouldn't be.

A similar and equally enjoyable comparison can be drawn using city populations. Using the United States Census Bureau's 2020 Census Data[26], New York City's population currently stands at 8.8 million people (presumably the United States Census Bureau is more dependable than the National Weather Service?). It would take another 33 New York City populations before you even get to the 1 in 292,000,000 odds to win Powerball's jackpot. Imagine New York City's population times 33. That's a lot of Ubers and taxis. And trash. My goodness, the trash.

Here's some more info to spew out at your next cocktail party. To get to those 1 in 292,000,000 million Powerball odds you would need:

- 29 Los Angeleses (population of 10 million[27])
- 108 Chicagos (population 2.7 million[28])
- 126 Houstons (population of 2.3 million[29])
- 660 Miamis (population of 440,000[30])

---

[26] https://data.census.gov/all?q=New+York+City

[27] https://data.census.gov/all?q=Los+Angeles

[28] https://data.census.gov/all?q=Chicago

[29] https://data.census.gov/all?q=Houston

[30] https://data.census.gov/all?q=miami,+FL

- • 447 Portland ORs (population of 652,000[31])
- • 4,268 Portland MEs (population of 68,000[32])
- • 14,325 Portland TXs (population of 20,300[33])
- • 10.4 million Portland IAs (population of 20)

Durango Bill describes lottery odds in a very sobering perspective on his website[34]. In this example pulled from his site, he writes about the odds for Mega Millions glory:

The average return per $2.00 ticket includes the extremely low probability that you might win a large prize – for example $10,000 or more. As a practical matter, it is unlikely that you will ever buy enough tickets (fork out enough money) to ever have much of a chance for any of the large prizes. Thus it is probable that all you will ever get back from your ticket purchases are piddling small amounts. The percentages for these small amounts can be calculated. The table below shows the percentage chances for various "piddling returns."

If you spend $1,000 to buy 500 tickets (= 1 ticket for each of 500 Mega Millions games = 1 ticket per Mega Millions game, 2 times a week for 4.8 years) there is a:

- - *49.79 % chance that you will get back $64 or less*
- - *58.41 % chance that you will get back $68 or less*
- - *69.82 % chance that you will get back $74 or less*
- - *78.81 % chance that you will get back $80 or less*
- - *89.56 % chance that you will get back $92 or less*
- - *94.96 % chance that you will get back $116 or*

---

[31] https://data.census.gov/all?q=portland,+oregon
[32] https://data.census.gov/all?q=portland,+me

[33] https://data.census.gov/all?q=Portland+city,+Texas

[34] https://www.durangobill.com/MegaMillionsOdds.html

> *less*
> - *98.04 % chance that you will get back $280 or less*
> - *99.02 % chance that you will get back $554 or less*
> - *99.52 % chance that you will get back $572 or less*
> - *99.90 % chance that you will get back $750 or less*
>
> *Even if you buy 500 tickets, your chance of winning $10,000 or a larger prize is less than 1 in 1,000.*

Another amusing way to think about lottery odds comes courtesy of Matthew Kovach, an assistant professor of economics at Virginia Tech. In a story[35] published on January 14, 2023 by USA Today, he said:

> *"Imagine you write the letters to 'Mega Millions' on individual pieces of paper, mix them up, and let your cat randomly select letters. Your cat is five times more likely to correctly spell 'Mega Millions' than you are to win."*

If you've got a cat, enjoy that activity. Put it on YouTube and go viral!

Don't get too discouraged! There is a way to guarantee that you hit the jackpot. Now, aren't you glad you bought this book? The answer to all of your dreams is right here. Ready?

Your path to financial glory lies with Dr. Mark Glickman, a Fellow of the American Statistical Association and Senior Lecturer on Statistics at the Harvard University Department

---

[35] https://www.usatoday.com/story/news/nation/2023/01/14/mega-millions-drawing-winning-ticket-1-35-billion-sold-maine/11040405002/

of Statistics, and an elected member of the American Statistical Association's Board of Directors. He is also a tournament chess player, where he attained the title of U.S. national master in 1988 and is known for having invented the Glicko and Glicko-2 rating systems, both adopted by many gaming organizations throughout the world, particularly online.

When I spoke with him, Glickman told me that "One possible strategy is that if you had the resources to do so, you could actually buy every single combination. That's it. I think it's like 292 million or so combinations at $2 per ticket. So if your outlay would be just under $600 million for the tickets and the jackpot is $1.2 billion, you've basically guaranteed that you're going to be able to win it. That sounds good at first glance, but of course, the problem is that these games are parimutuel games, meaning that if it's multiple winners, you split the money evenly."

So here is problem #1. This will only work if a) the jackpot is very high and b) you are the only winner. The former is obviously something you can identify by just looking at the numbers. The latter makes this strategy a tremendous risk. And that's only problem #1.

"Right," says Glickman. "So if you have this idea that you're going to buy every single ticket, laying out your 600 million to guarantee that you're going to win the jackpot, then perhaps a lot of other people are, too. Then you'll see those diminishing returns really quickly."

And what about the two payout options? If you take the cash upfront option, that cuts the advertised prize roughly in half. So you'd have to take the prize in annual installments over 30 years.

"And not even then," adds Glickman, citing what is now problem #2. "I'm not even sure that works out. I mean, you have to start fiddling with numbers and doing these computations where, you know, there's the present value of today's money, but the value is actually going to decrease over time. So, in fact, you're not actually getting even that amount of money. And I know you're going to bring up the taxes, too."

Ah yes. Problem #3. Taxes. Federal and state taxes will also take at least 37% of your profit away, and likely more than that, depending on where you live. The obvious question is emerging—is this strategy dumb?

"It's hugely risky. I mean, unless you're somebody like Elon Musk where losing a couple of hundred million is not really going to impact your life at all, you're taking a huge risk by doing this because the only way this gives you any chance at making a lot of money is that you actually have to buy a lot of tickets." Glickman then adds, "You don't have to buy all the tickets in order for this type of strategy to work. But you're going to have to buy, you know, at least upwards of like 30% of the tickets for this type of strategy to really give you any chance at winning."

Hold on! You don't have to buy all of the tickets to have a good chance at winning?

"What's actually interesting is that we have that basic strategy—just buy them all. But it also kind of works if you scale back the total jackpot and the amount of tickets you're willing to buy." He goes on to explain that if the jackpot isn't too big, there will be fewer people buying tickets. This means that you could still end up buying a lot of tickets but you don't have to buy every combination to have a reasonable chance."

He continues, "So there's some jackpot dollar amount where that kind of strategy actually will work. I mean, not to buy *all* the tickets, but like some number where your chances are kind of optimized. And that's something that - in principle - one could figure out if you actually had enough information on how many people were participating on a day-by-day basis as a function of what the prize money was. If you're buying 30% of the tickets, you're spending roughly $200 million. Those are dollars you're going to have to outlay where there's a real chance you're not going to win. I mean, you have to be kind of comfortable losing $1,000,000."

Glickman then adds some more mind-bending food for thought.

"There's something called the 'Law of Large Numbers,' which sounds like a goofy name, but it's actually the technical name for the probability that if you repeat this kind of experiment in the long run, the odds will end up being in your favor. So if you did figure out that optimal point and you were willing to lose $200 million every once in a while and play the lottery with some reasonable frequency, in the end, it'll work out for you and you'll get some real money."

So, who's willing to lose $200 million every once in a while? Seems do-able for the average Joes like us, right? That's a world that seems hard to fathom. Has anyone actually attempted any of this before?

"Apparently there was this guy in Texas who owned a big restaurant chain and he ended up buying 50,000 tickets with the promise that if he won he would divide the money equally among all of his employees. And I think that business was around 10,000 employees nationwide," said Glickman.

He is referring to the CEO of the Raising Canes restaurant chain based in Texas, who did in fact spend $100,000 for 50,000 Mega Millions tickets and vowed to split the winning jackpot of $810 million with all his employees.

In a statement Graves published prior to the lottery, he wrote, "As soon as we heard how big this jackpot prize is, we couldn't miss out on the chance to win the Mega Millions jackpot and share it with our crew, who always stand together. None of what we do at Cane's would be possible without our crew, which is why we are always looking for ways to bring them a little extra fun, and if we're lucky, a surprise on Wednesday morning."

While you wonder about the percent volume increase in job applications to Raising Canes during that time period, consider the result: "Yeah, he didn't win," mused Glickman, with a smile on his face.

There is also a notion that the more you play, the less chance you have to win. And it's somewhat logical at first glance. The more Bryant-Denny stadiums you pile on top of each other, the smaller chance you have to win, right? That's actually true, because the stadium example is a random drawing for one single winner. A person's name. This isn't exactly true with games like Powerball and Mega Millions, as there is a finite amount of numbers to play, as Dr. Glickman mentioned.

"Your odds of winning never change because the numbers are the numbers. They're actually random. So the only thing that you could strategize and the only thing that you have any control over is understanding what types of numbers other people pick. People will end up typically picking birthdays or some other numbers that might be kind of common or look like patterns that they'll trace out. Avoid patterns. The best strategy is just to do a quick pick, completely random because that's going to make it less likely that you're going to be part of any pattern."

The only odds that change with more people playing are the odds that you'll have to share the prize with more people.

With all statistical indications showing that it is not entirely smart to play the lottery regardless of buying 1 ticket or 292,000,000 tickets, does a Fellow of the American Statistical Association and Senior Lecturer on Statistics at the Harvard University Department of Statistics play the lottery much? No way, right?

Dr. Glickman laughs. "I play the lottery when the jackpot gets sky high, but even then, maybe five tickets. I'm doing it for fun and not strategizing. It's just sort of a fun thing to play every once in a while. And thank you for reminding me, because the Mega Millions is $800 million tonight."

Nobody won that night, by the way.

So it's simple, right? If you want a guaranteed win, just buy every possible number combination. To take this on just to hope you don't have to split the jackpot, I'm not sure it's worth it. You'd need a lot of time, a whole lot of money, and a whole bunch of stupidity, because even if you buy every combination, it remains an incredibly sizable risk.

It may indeed get you on the news, though. There's always that.

CHAPTER THREE

James Hayes

In 1966, James Hayes was 12 years old and had already experienced things no child should ever have to. His biological father was absent from the opening bell. His mother re-married, but James was taken from the family at the age of 12 and placed into foster care for nearly a month.

It is well studied and documented by child psychiatrists, pediatric doctors and behavioral scientists that those early childhood years are absolutely crucial to the core shaping of a human being and play a large part in the formation of human tendencies. In terms of finances, for example, there are plenty of basic lessons to teach young children about the value of saving, budgeting, and spending money. It's safe to say that James's early childhood was filled with uncertainty, instability, and the occasional crisis. This didn't allow much time for learning about financial responsibility and many other important, foundational life lessons.

I talked with the animated and affable Hayes for many hours in separate Zoom and phone conversations during the winter of 2023. In talking about his early childhood, he explains he was taken from his house at the age of 12 because of child abuse and placed into foster care. He wouldn't be there for long.

"My grandmother came and adopted me. From there it was a pretty strict upbringing. If she had taught me to swim, she would have just thrown me in the deep end and let me figure it out! She was old-school like that. The house she grew up in had a dirt floor. Because of that, she saved every penny and she was very frugal, but not cheap. And she was very smart with her money. What made her most comfortable was just looking at the bank statements each month to see what the numbers said. It's all about perspective."

Upon being adopted by his grandmother Melba Hayes, James settled into life in Camarillo, California, tucked into a coastal plain between scenic mountains and beaches. In the mid-1950s, the Ventura Freeway (the 101) was built, starting in Los Angeles and heading north, which made the trip from L.A. up to Camarillo an easy one-hour drive. The new freeway meant population growth and typical-of-the-time suburban sprawl. It also meant cars of all types cruising up the 101 North into Camarillo during a time when the car culture in the U.S. was at its peak.

"I've always been into cars and racing...I remember watching the Indianapolis 500 every year. I watched the 1969 Indy 500 with my stepfather when Mario Andretti won it. Mario became my hero right then and there. He's so decorated and so famous, like the Michael Jordan of car racing. He was like a god to me."

So things began to stabilize a little for James. His grandmother provided comfort, not excess. Reliability, not unpredictability. Stability, not uncertainty. It can be argued that beyond a shadow of a doubt, James Hayes's grandmother saved his life. Still, those first 12 years are important in the shaping of a growing mind, the building of a child's foundation, and the nurturing that sets the tone for the remainder of one's life. And it largely wasn't there for him before his adoption.

His grandmother instilled some passions that he maintains today.

"Two things I've always loved: cars and music. I was in the orchestra and played the violin as a kid. I really bonded with music early. I'm actually the youngest person ever inducted into the Ventura County Orchestra as a violinist at the age of 13! And I always had the fastest car on this side of town in my teens."

There's a detectable pride in his voice as he says it.Alas, 13 is a pivotal age. The following years are well-known as years of rapid growth, both physical and mental. As teens develop the ability to think more abstractly, they also start thinking more philosophically, more politically, and more longer-term. Socially, as so many have experienced, it can be a mental minefield with the incessant comparing of one's self to peers, acceptance from others, and the gradual seeking of independence from parents. Or grandparents, in this case. Self-esteem starts to either grow stronger or weaker. James has a more simple description of this time.

"I turned 14 or 15 and was getting interested in girls. I noticed very quickly that if you carried around a violin case, girls would run the other way! So that was pretty much the end of me playing the violin." His contagious laughter fills the kitchen as he says this.

"I had a lot of freedom others didn't. I started ditching school and did a lot of stupid shit. I still loved music, just in a different way. And I never did finish high school."

His self-described stupid shit never included disrespecting or defying his grandmother, though. James recalls one particular moment when things got tense.

"On the day I turned 18, Nana called me into the living room and handed me a stack of envelopes. It was a stack of bills! I was so mad at her for two weeks and then I realized she was teaching me a lesson." He paid the bills.

Even after this bumpy lesson, James and his grandma maintained a close relationship and as James aged into his 20's, they started playing the lottery together.

"We played twice a week for 11 years. Every week…we never missed buying a ticket, from 1987 on!"

Dropping out of high school pushed James into the workforce and he became a faithful, dependable employee at Dial Security, a company that installed security systems for residential and industrial buildings. Here was yet another opportunity for James to learn from his grandmother—go for the reliable, stable paycheck.

"I worked my way up in security for Dial. Started when I was 18 and stayed…until I was 34." Holding down a job at the same place for that amount of time safely assumes that Dial had a very dedicated employee who did his job well. Bill Dundas was James's boss at Dial.

"Jim was a good employee," Dundas explained, "he was professional in the work that he performed and was always friendly and outgoing."

Meanwhile, James and his Nana continued buying lottery tickets. Twice a week, every week. When asked if there was ever much discussion of what they would do if they actually won, James cheekily responds.

"Not really. We just played. We hit 5 out of 6 one time and I thought we were gonna get a couple hundred thousand—it blew my mind! We only got $40 bucks because a bunch of other people hit it at the same time too. I was so pissed at the lottery that day," he laughs.

He may not have been discussing winning much with Melba, but in 11 years of buying lottery tickets, he did allow his mind to bounce around the idea of winning.

"Always dreamed of a house on the beach and a Lamborghini. I always had faith that before they put me in the ground, I was going to own a Lambo. I didn't know how, but I knew that Lambo was going to happen. You can bend the laws of God—but not break them—with faith. It's simple: don't buy lottery tickets if you don't think you're gonna win. If you don't believe in it, don't do it."

He believed. And on January 7, 1998, everything changed.

"I bought my lottery ticket as usual in the morning on the way to work, but then I spent an extra 5 dollars on an extra ticket. I had put that $5 in my pocket for coffee and a donut for after work, like I always did. As I was pumping my gas that morning, a little voice inside me said I should go back in and buy one more. The voice was saying 'You gotta go buy one more right now! But then I kept telling myself that I already bought one when I got my OJ and cigarettes! But I went back in and I bought one more."

That one was the winner.

"I do believe in luck. I think everyone has had beginner's luck. Luck is real. I know Lady Luck's biggest secret, though —you make your luck," he stresses. "What you do puts you in a position to be lucky. My Nana taught me that. We have to live it to learn it!"

James Hayes played the lottery every day, ten dollars a week for 11 years. That's roughly $5,700 invested in a game with little-to-no odds of winning. And he sure made his luck. The jackpot that day was $19 million dollars, which is around $34 million in 2023's money. But nothing can be that easy, especially in James' life.

"Let me tell you something," he says, about a solitary moment one week before he won. "It was midnight on New Year's Eve, '97 into '98. I was sitting in my bedroom and I had married this girl I was going out with. She was 18 and I was 34. I had made a big mistake and I knew it. She turned from Dr. Jekyll right into Mr. Hyde. She was disrespecting my grandma, first of all. That's enough right there. But it was more than that. I owed the IRS $250 bucks, my car needed $300 in repairs and I just remember praying 'God get me out of this pickle.' I wasn't even praying for lottery money or anything, just praying in general. I was already thinking about how I was going to divorce her. Then a week later I was a multi-millionaire."

Hayes remembers the moment he learned he had won with stunning clarity.

"I came home after a 12-hour night shift and Nana was awake reading the paper and watching TV. I gave her the lottery ticket because I was tired and I just went to bed. She woke me up at some point and said it was on the news that the winning ticket was purchased at the USA Central gas station and she thinks we won. I was like 'Holy shit!' So I was excited but still had my doubts. I didn't have that moment where you shit your pants; that happened later," he says, with that infectious laugh.

"I was fortunate enough that the $5 quick pick I bought, that extra ticket, made me a winner. I told Nana that I had to go to the California State Lottery office and that there was gonna be news media there, so I asked her if she wanted to go with me. She said no, that I should go on my own. I remember asking her if she wanted a new car or a new couch, or anything. She said no! She was telling me that she was already familiar with her car and that she knew where all the buttons and controls were and that her couch was already broken in and comfortable. She didn't want anything except for one thing: for me to be there every night."

James called his brother, who didn't believe him, and the two drove to the California State Lottery. The office was closed so they went out for an anxiety-filled breakfast. When enough time had passed, the pair went back to the lottery office. The lottery employee put the ticket in the machine and it came out confirmed as the winner.

"He told me that I better sign it. I asked him how much I had won and he said it was at least $11 million. That's when I shit myself," James laughs again.

"Then we sat there for a couple of hours because they had to call in the security guy at the lottery, who had to interview me for official confirmation."

Imagine. You have just been told you are a multi-millionaire, and now you have to sit at the lottery office for hours waiting…waiting…waiting. What goes through your mind? Is it even real? It has to be the slowest consecutive hours a person will ever experience—worse than the DMV. With all kinds of scenarios swimming frantically in their head. Losing the ticket. Having a heart attack right there. A random asteroid getting dropped on lottery headquarters. Earth blowing up. Surreal.

"So the security guy starts to interview me and says I'm probably gonna get a lot of weirdos contacting me. And death threats. All I asked was when I'll get the money! That's when I learned that the Lottery Commission has to do background checks to see if you owe the state or the government anything because they'll take that out before cutting a check. Then he said it'll probably be a couple of months before the first payment hit and right away I was like 'What the fuck? I'm gonna be poor for another couple of months?'"

If sitting in the lottery office feels long, imagine waiting for months for that first check!

"You know what else was funny about the security guy? He kept asking me multiple times where I bought the ticket. And if I knew the person who sold it to me. And he just kept asking me over and over if I could recall anything strange happening at all when I was buying the ticket. I finally said, "Yes, something strange did actually happen—I fucking won!"

That surreal day also meant the option of a news conference.

"I remember asking 'this is just for me?'" Hayes laughs. "Then my brother started talking about how this was my Andy Warhol '15 Minutes of Fame' and he told me I should do the news conference. I clearly remember him saying 'Look at that crack through the door. They're waiting for YOU!'"

James Hayes walked through that door and nothing was ever the same again.

"I felt like a movie star, everyone asking me questions. I answered 3 or 4 reporters at the press conference, but I only wanted to answer the pretty blonde reporter. Somebody asked me what I was going to do with the money and I said I was just going to help family and friends in need. I think saying that was one of the biggest mistakes I've ever made.

"I tell you what, though, I found out real quick how many *family* members I had across the country. And *friends*! That's a whole 'nother thing," Hayes said, with real emphasis and plenty of sarcasm.

"Imagine this," Hayes says, "you are nobody on January 6th; you've got a few friends, some family, and a small circle of people you know. Next day you're on the front page of the L.A. Times. I was right there, near another story about the Unabomber who had tried to commit suicide! Suddenly it seemed everyone knew who I was and had an opinion. It took me years to deal with that."

* * *

Photos by AYNE CUSACK / Los Angeles Times

Robert Wallace, center, of the USA gas station and Bob Stillman of the lottery office put up a "Millionaire Made Here" sign.

Newfound Security

Guard Business Was His Job, but $19-Million Jackpot Will Change That

By NICK GREEN
SPECIAL TO THE TIMES

C AMARILLO—James Hayes woke up a multimillionaire Thursday morning.

The 35-year-old Camarillo resident learned that he won $19 million in the SuperLotto jackpot just hours after he had finished his graveyard shift as a security guard supervisor.

It didn't take Hayes long to adjust to his new life.

He plans to buy a new car. He is already house hunting in Camarillo's ritzy Spanish Hills development. And, he has given his two weeks' notice to quit his job.

"Wouldn't you?" said a smirking Hayes.

"I'm not going to blow the money," he added. "I know I'll change. But only for the better. . . . Mainly what I want to do is help out my family and friends in need."

Hayes, the second-largest Ventura County lottery winner ever. will receive annual payments of $684,000 after taxes for the next 20 years. Oxnard resident Dolores Trejo became the

James Hayes bought ticket; wife Stephanie helps hold check.

county's biggest winner one year ago this month. when she pocketed a $34-million jackpot.

"It's kinda hard to grasp, but it's a lot." Hayes said of his winnings. "I've had a string of bad luck lately."

Please see LOTTERY, B5

Los Angeles Times, Friday, January 9, 1998

The next phase of James Hayes's life as a millionaire had begun. At Dial Security, he was making $36,000 per year. On January 7, his lottery salary was $684,000 per year, after taxes. Quietly and retrospectively, Hayes says "Before they give you a dime, they should make the winners take a class about money management. Same with getting married," he adds with a hearty laugh.

"Lots of lottery winners don't even know they're liable for taxes later. My mindset was 'I'm a millionaire, I do whatever I want now.'"

One of the first things he set his sights on was a Porsche. The lamborghini could wait. Before he won, James would often visit the local Porsche dealership, just to look at the beautiful sports cars. The staff there became familiar with this dreamer. "I promised I wouldn't touch one, but I also told them that someday I'd get one," he cracked, "they always just told me 'yeah right, kid.'"

So Hayes went back to Rusnak Porsche in Thousand Oaks, CA the day after the news conference. Armed with winnings, dying to spend his newfound riches, and quite eager to prove a bunch of Porsche staff wrong, he walked in with his head held high. He knew exactly which model he wanted.

On this day, however, they didn't have the model he wanted in stock, and the staff wrote it off as just another visit from the dreamer who'd never buy one anyway. As fate would have it, his lottery news conference aired on the TV news in the dealership. A coincidence of coincidences. On his way to the Porsche dealership, Hayes had driven by the Chevy place and saw the brand new C5 Corvette Convertible on display, so he told the Rusnak staff that he would just head back down there to get it. With multiple sets of eyeballs darting back and forth from the person on the television to the person who was standing in front of them, things got a lot more accommodating for Hayes.

"They said 'Oh wait wait. The owner wants to meet you!' And this guy comes out and he looks like he's in the mafia, got a cigar in his mouth, and he says 'hey kid' and invites me in his office for some champagne and we sit down and he asks me 'Do you buy your suits off the rack?' and I told him I don't even own a suit! Then he tells me that now I'm gonna have a tailor. And then he says to me 'Let's order you a Turbo' and then I tell him I just want black everything inside and out with whatever the best materials are. And I got out of there as quick as I could because I was getting a car *today*. Long story short, I went down and bought that Corvette," he chuckles.

Five months later Rusnak Porsche called to let James know his all-black car had arrived. He had forgotten that he actually ordered it. He had the Corvette, had also added his long-wanted Lamborghini, and owned a pickup truck for good measure. It may indeed be hard to imagine how someone could forget ordering a Porsche as well. But it's also hard to imagine an 1800% increase in income overnight.

Then Hayes throws this gem in, "Then they said if you get here quickly Richie Sambora and Heather Locklear will be there picking theirs up, too!"

Music and cars. Two passions of James Hayes.

"It normally takes about 30 minutes to get to Rusnak from my grandma's house. I made it in 20 minutes," Hayes says with that laugh. "The brakes were smoking. So me and my brother are there and Richie is talking to me, checking out my Lamborghini and my brother is just checking out Heather Locklear, you know? But that's how my life was, it was all just a blur."

It wasn't all laughs, though. Hayes started getting death threats a mere few weeks after he won. One came in the form of a letter, as if straight out of a Hollywood production. It was a ransom-style note with letters cut out of magazines that spelled out the threats. Another writer claimed to be a high school classmate of Hayes, telling him that he had known

James since high school, hated him then, hated him now and that he would kill James if he saw him.

This experience is common across the country, and aside from being terrifying, raises a new question: Why do some states require winners to reveal their names to the public? There is a large contingent of people across the world who are desperate for money. Some may be mentally ill. Some may be facing a health crisis. Some may just be in it for a lark. A lottery winner is seen as a tremendous opportunity for these people. But Hayes's experience was no different than the thousands of other publicly-exposed winners who were subject to email, phone calls, and even house visits.

One in particular sticks with him even now.

"This one is hard to talk about," says Hayes, as his infectious laugh fades into the background.

"About two weeks after I won I was sitting in my garage one night, just staring at my Corvette. Big smile on my face. I heard something on the porch, then the doorbell rang. It was 10:30 at night." He grabbed his Smith & Wesson and tucked it in the back of his waistband. He opened the door and was greeted by a man standing on his porch with two little girls. The girls are both sobbing. "He asks me 'Are you James Hayes?' and I said 'Who wants to know?'"

Hayes' voice drops and I feel the weight of this moment hit me.

"He told me that he had AIDS from a blood transfusion and that he would die soon and he wanted me to take his two daughters so they would have a good life. I told him to get the fuck off my property."

Hayes wipes tears from his eyes as he adds, "I've regretted that to this day and I wonder all the time about those kids and what happened to them."

He collects himself for a moment and then tries to put it into perspective. "You have to understand, I was getting hundreds of letters per day, like right away. In California, if you had something like 6 pounds or more of mail, they wouldn't deliver it, you had to pick it up, so I had to go to the post office every day to get piles and piles of letters, asking me for money. I was getting calls, letters, everything. It was overwhelming. I gave some money to family, gave some to a few friends but then some people came back for more. And more. And more. I had to start saying no."

After a minute to collect himself, Hayes perks up a little. "My favorite one was the five letters I got, all from the same lady. She just put naked pictures of herself in the envelope. What?" His laugh returns.

The slow descent of Hayes's winnings began with making good on his pre-win vow to end his very short marriage to Stephanie. They bought a house soon after winning and tried to make things work, but he had barely stepped into the new house before she was arrested for spousal abuse. James moved back in with Melba and the divorce was finalized in 1999. It was the right decision, but hacked a sizable amount of money away from his winnings.

"In California, half of whatever you have goes to the spouse automatically," Hayes ruefully says. "Also, I had made sure that half of that lottery money was my grandmother's. We negotiated with Stephanie and she ended up with 25% of the total winnings. Half of my half. She became an official California state lottery winner and got her checks right from the state after that."

Hayes wouldn't be single for long. In another odd coincidence, the woman who would become his second wife was also named Stephanie.

"Stephanie #2 and I had been friends for years before I won. I think she was 15 and I was maybe 19 when we met. I was friends with her older brother and on Halloween night she came to my door with a few of her friends. She had roller skates on and was basically dressed like a Playboy bunny. I couldn't keep my eyes off her! We really clicked and she was actually good friends with my girlfriend at the time. I broke up with that girl to start dating Stephanie. Those were really the happiest years of my life. We had a lot of fun and we went through a lot of tough times."

The new century brought both heartbreak and elation for Hayes in a short period of time. On January 1, 2000, Melba Hayes, the person who brought stability and levity to James's life for twenty-plus years, passed away. The blow of losing his grandmother was softened a little on February 14, 2000, when James and Stephanie were married. Hayes cheekily adds that he loved that date, not because of its implied romanticism, but because he could easily remember his anniversary each year. He also started working with an accountant who explained the importance of buying a house, saving him a lot of money in lottery-tax liability. Buying a $2 million dollar house would mean paying $6000 a month in deductible interest, which would more-or-less offset the liability he owed.

"So I bought the $2 million dollar house," he said, "lived there for 1.5 to 2 years, then sold it for $3 million. If I had only stayed there and bought nothing new…," he trails off for a second. "It sold for $8 million recently," he adds.

It was now time for another Lamborghini. To nobody's surprise, he went all-out and purchased a very rare model that qualified him for the "Running of the Bulls," a fundraiser for the California Highway Patrol Foundation, helping members of the CHP and their families. In short, a group of Lamborghini owners all get together and collectively drive from Newport Beach to Monterey, CA. Hayes was going to make the drive. If that wasn't exciting enough for him, none other than Mario Andretti, his boyhood hero, would be driving the lead car. James Hayes, the $17.50 per hour security worker turned millionaire, would be driving with Andretti up the California coast. A dream truly come true.

Hayes remembers it fondly and clearly.

"I go with my best friend Jim and all the cars are laid out, like 50 Lambos. Mine has an $18,000 optional paint job, candy magenta with purple. The Speed Channel is filming! Then I see Mario standing there looking at my car! I got to meet Mario Andretti. I shook his hand and told him how I watched him win Indy when I was 8. Mario liked my Lambo better and he asked me if he could drive mine! It was more incredible than winning $19 million dollars! It was so surreal. I was the #2 car right behind Mario!"

Hayes looks back on those few years with Stephanie in their beautiful $2 million home with glowing sentiment, but recognition of the ups and downs along the way. "I lived my dream! Every fantasy in my head that I wanted to. At the end of the day, you have to look inside yourself and ask what is going to make me happy. I just wanted one good woman to love me for me—and you can't buy that. I had it! The most important things in life have nothing to do with money. The most valuable thing is your brain. And your word. Then it's your time. We don't know how much time we have. I place a high value on everyone's time now, not just mine.

"I've learned in 60 years that everything is duality. The yin. The yang. Everything in the universe works on balance. There's all these paradoxes. I don't like them! Here's an example. I had a custom license plate on my Lamborghini and it said 'ULOSE TO' which has something to do with drag racing. One day a guy came up to me and was being really snotty and called me an asshole. Said that just because I won the lottery, I assumed everyone else was a loser. He thought I was showing off my lottery winnings because of my license plate. It really changed my perspective about judging people's dreams."

* * *

The "ULOSE TO" license plate. Photo courtesy of James Hayes

* * *

James Hayes, left, with Mario Andretti. Photo courtesy of James Hayes

The yin and the yang kept right on pulsing and stretching out to further and further extremes.The yang: Hayes finally had the loving relationship he craved, topped off with a nice house on the beach and some good advice from an accountant. These were some of his best years, and although his money was starting to dwindle to lower levels, he was enjoying a bit of the high life and taking advantage of his stunning lottery luck.

The yin is a story that sadly befell thousands of people in the early 2000s and turned out to be the event that truly began Hayes's spiral downward. He was injured in an accident in 1999 (he declined to provide details) and after some time had passed, the physical after-effects of the accident necessitated doctors putting him on a series of painkillers, which eventually ended up being the new revolutionary medication called…Oxycontin. It's not hard to figure out where this story goes.

At the time, Oxy was heralded by its manufacturer, Purdue Pharma, as a new phenomenon in pain management, but has since become a pivotal point in BigPharma's history. It's almost darkly absurd to think back to a time when Oxycontin was thought of and pitched as a non-addictive miracle drug. Of course, now we know that all of it was a gigantic lie, perpetuated by frothy Purdue marketing and sales staff. All things Oxy have been covered ad nauseam by a myriad of news outlets, books, and streaming TV series. It does not bear any further expansion here.

Hayes explains that after his accident, his doctors put him on pain management. "It started with Vicodin and then you just build a tolerance to that, so they start giving you other stuff. It all just keeps getting stronger and stronger and stronger instead of them just saying 'Hold on, it looks like maybe these aren't working for you.' But they just kept scaling me up. Worked my way up to prescribed oxycontin to the point where a traumatic event happened."

More on that soon.

Years passed. More money was spent. More painkillers. More Oxy. Tolerance to the drug grew. Then Stephanie encountered some tragic events in a very short time period— her brother, her father, and her best friend all passed away within months of each other. She spiraled into depression and could not cope. On top of that, a history of headaches and migraines was exacerbated by this string of awful deaths. The drugs her husband was taking offered a respite, and both of them were now in deep.

"We were both doing drugs," Hayes says, "a lot." He mentions that some people close to Stephanie blame him for this, but Hayes offers a different take.

"I didn't push drugs on her ever, but we were married. They were there. She was taking drugs with me because of chronic headaches and migraines so she could feel better. Me and Stephanie had a really good marriage."

But the money was running out. Cars were sold. The house was sold. Hayes laments about the last Lamborghini he owned. "It was actually in the Busta Rhymes/Mariah Carey video 'I Know What You Want.' I sat there and smoked weed with Busta and watched Mariah yell at her stylist about having the wrong shorts or some shit." He laughs heartily.

Any light was softly and slowly fading to dark. James, sensing a catastrophically blown opportunity as a lottery winner, also sank into depression. Which made the drugs more and more appealing, dulling the physical and mental pain. Their growing endurance to the painkillers fueled a drug habit that vacuumed up what little money they had left. While the big wigs at Purdue Pharma were setting sail on yachts and showing Wall Street astronomical quarterly earnings, James, Stephanie, and so many others in the United States were falling apart on Main Street.

An investor stepped in and helped Hayes buy an apartment building, providing work and a place to live. Things were okay for a while until more bad luck struck—the building was destroyed by fire. Cause unknown.

"I got everyone out," Hayes says very proudly, "lots of smoke damage, everyone displaced and pretty much homeless. California law said we had to pay two months of rent to every tenant. Almost everything I had was tied up in that building and business, and I was unable to pay the insurance premiums. Hell, I couldn't even afford my medicine. I wasn't ever a drug addict before, but now I was, all from this prescribed medicine," he adds.

It was now 2015 and James Hayes was homeless.

"So I'm now living in a garage, broke as a joke, and had sold all my valuable things. Was driving a crappy Volkswagen Rabbit. Scraping to survive. I had applied to something like 34 places to work and had 2 interviews. I hadn't worked in 20 years! I even went to Mcdonalds and all they said was 'We only have high school kids who work here.' And I looked around and pointed right over to someone behind the counter and I said 'There's an older woman working right there!' and all they told me was that it was a token elderly person. 'Every fast food joint has one,' they said."

Hayes went back to Dial Security, where he worked dependably for 15 years prior to winning. They took him back. But it didn't last long.

"They gave me my old job back for a year," he says. "The thing was, I was kind of burning the candle at both ends and so we just mutually parted ways."

Bill Dundas, his old boss, was still at Dial. "Yes, he came back and worked for a while. He presented well and that's all I'm going to say," Dundas said, very curt and short. He declined to comment any further.

Hayes was unable to find ways to support his now $2000+ a month reliance on Oxycontin. Any attempt to wean off the drug was followed by such horrendous sickness that any other basic duties of life would stop dead in their tracks. Hayes, a winner of $19 million in the California state lottery in 1998, was homeless, broke, and addicted. But the story gets even worse, and it's one that was very common in Oxycontin's heyday.

"A friend told me I was in withdrawal and recommended heroin. I had never done that. He said he could get me $20 worth that would set me up for weeks. At first, I said no, but I got sicker and sicker from the Oxy withdrawal and finally gave up. I didn't know what to do.

The heroin solved the sickness and now the monkey was on my back. To me, the pills and the heroin weren't that much different. I found myself stuck on heroin now. It was a piece of the puzzle. I needed money for rent, I needed money for a car, I needed money for drugs. Unemployment denied me any support because the apartment building business didn't pay into the system. They said I was an independent contractor. I appealed and they denied me.

"Now it's June 2016 and I couldn't get a job, didn't know what to do, and now I'm doing heroin so I don't get sick," he says with incredulousness, "I feel like a loser. I had it all, it was all right there, and I lost it all. But when you're at the top, there's only one way to go. Back down."

But even that wasn't the bottom.

"You can put this in your book," laughs Hayes as he talks about what happened halfway through 2016. "I blame Judas Priest. Music has always been a go-to thing for me. I had my little earbuds in and I happened to be listening to their well-known song 'Breaking the Law' and after I listened to it, I thought *that's me right now*."

"Those lyrics resonated in my head," he said. "I had no choice but to look at the option of breaking the law. I'd always been a law-abiding citizen. I feel like I'm a good guy, I'd never been arrested or anything. No criminal record. Zero. And if I'm going to target someone, that narrows down the list of things I can do. I would never steal a stereo out of someone's car or grab an old lady's purse. So I couldn't hurt or rob individuals. I can't do that. But I was a fan of bank robbery movies my whole life, you know, John Dillinger and the whole thing. You gotta have balls and you gotta be crazy, and I had both of those things."

So Hayes made a decision—he was going to rob a bank, the logic being that he was going against The Establishment and not a person. Hayes cites a book he'd read called *Where the Money Is: True Tales from the Bank Robbery Capital of the World* by FBI Special Agent William J. Rehder. The book detailed the lives and crimes of bank robbers in modern-day Los Angeles. It was in this book that Hayes discovered that the statute of limitation for bank robbery was only five years. That piqued his interest.

"They say that for bank robberies, there's a magic two minutes—if you can get out and get away in two minutes, you're good. I thought I could get it to four minutes. The more I researched it, the more I thought I could do it. I knew I was slick enough to do one or two banks and they would never catch me. So I studied the book and planned. I would try to hit them as close to five o'clock as possible because I knew that's when cops were changing shifts, which meant there was a better chance they'd be farther away."

Hayes went to a small handful of banks to observe them, including the Montecito Bank & Trust. At first, he was nervous and scared. He was also backed into a corner.

"I finally got the balls to do one, the Montecito Bank and Trust. I remember standing out there contemplating it and I just went in and did it. It was so easy and so smooth. I actually had to stop the teller from giving me more money because I needed to get out fast, so I said 'that's enough!' I had an angel and a devil on my shoulder, just like Animal House! Next thing I know I'm driving down the freeway with $10,000 in cash." He laughs.

Hayes now had desperation and confidence; a dangerous combination. He began planning his next jobs. Plural.

"I went to my friend's barbershop and got all the discarded hair. I would leave those hairs at the next banks to mislead the FBI agents. One of the hairs even came back to a known felon!"

Hayes pauses for a moment and states again that while his

primary goal was to get money, he never intended or wanted to hurt anyone, but he would definitely rob more banks. Not one bank. Or two. Or even three. Hayes would go on to rob 10 more banks from April to September of 2017 and became known as the PT Cruiser Bandit, using that vehicle as the getaway car in several of the robberies.

In total, Hayes took just over $39,000 in the robberies according to U.S. Attorneys.

"I always smiled, I always walked out calmly. I had a disguise and I added some weight. I had an old shirt and some pillows, bought some makeup, made my face a little darker, and put on a grey-haired wig. I looked like a fat Eazy-E," he laughs uproariously at that comment, comparing himself to the well-known rapper.

"The others were all just a baseball cap and sunglasses and I kept my head down. I knew facial recognition wouldn't help anyway because I'd never been arrested. I changed to a fedora for one of them and there's a well-known photo of that one."

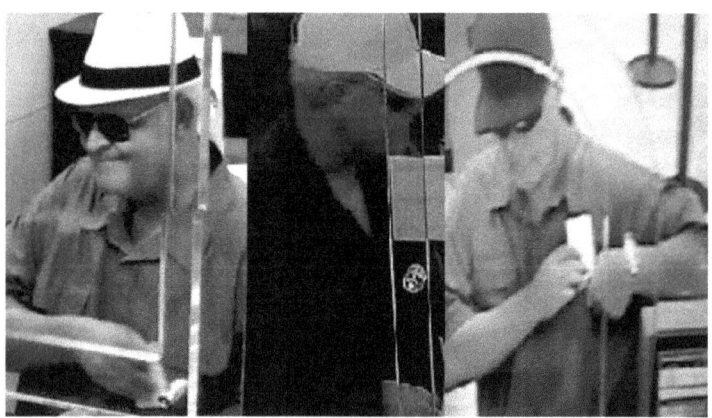

The FBI released these photos of James Hayes at the time of the robberies

* * *

Hayes gets reflective for a moment. "Those Judas Priest song lyrics were in my head. *Put some action in your life.* I really wrestled with my moral values. Truly. But it kept coming back to bank robbing. Honestly, after I got past the first two, it was more of a suicide mission and I just did riskier things. I even went to a Wells Fargo that I robbed already and it was the same teller as before. She just ran right back and pulled the alarm."

His PT Cruiser was identified in one of the robberies and that was the beginning of the end. The Santa Barbara Independent[36] reported the following:

The Montecito Bank & Trust in Carpinteria is the first bank Hayes is believed to have robbed; in his plea bargain, he admitted to four of the 10 robberies, though the same man appears in all surveillance videos. The cameras in Carpinteria taped a heavyset, middle-aged white man wearing black, a ballcap, and sunglasses. The same man appears on tape next at the Union Bank in Carpinteria on May 24, where he demanded, and received, $5,000, which he then used to buy a "light-colored PT Cruiser," according to court filings. That car was identified in the next robbery, of a Wells Fargo in Santa Clarita on June 12, in which his teller note stated he had a gun and to "be quick."

FBI investigator Ingerd Sotelo was able to zero in on Hayes after the tip came in, using data from a telecommunications search based on his address—the burned apartment building. The criminal complaint describes how the FBI had set up a license plate reader at a likely spot between the counties where the bank thefts were taking place. Sotelo located Hayes's gold PT Cruiser at the Castaic intersection after he tried to hit the Wells Fargo in Newhall a second time, but left after he was recognized.

---

[36] https://www.independent.com/2018/06/15/seasoned-bandit-said-suffer-lottery-curse/

* * *

The last bank he would hit, his 11th robbery, was the Union Bank in Pacific Palisades, CA. Then, finally, it was all over. He was tracked down and arrested by the FBI in October of 2018. Hayes was living in an abandoned garage with his wife, both of whom were destitute and addicted to drugs. He surrendered peacefully and without incident.

"My only play was to admit to everything right out of the gate because I knew it might help with my sentence. I asked for three things: a cigarette, a cherry coke, and to kiss my wife goodbye. They took me outside and I smoked the slowest cigarette of my life," Hayes laughs. "They gave me a cherry coke and they actually let me see Stephanie. She came I gave her a hug and a kiss. Then I told them everything."

Humans do odd, terrible, brave, creative, or dumb things when they are backed into a corner. James Hayes made bad decisions and he is the first to tell someone that. Hayes's life, however, had only seen small stretches of true stability. Winning the lottery did not provide stability for him. In fact, it could be argued that it made his life more unstable. He had tasted a few years with cash in his pocket and he bought a lot of cars and had a nice house, but those are just *things. Things* do not equal stability.

Consciously, Hayes had the math equation in his head: rob banks = get money = buy drugs = feel better.

Sub-consciously, though, the bank robbing was a true cry for help. Not for money or drugs, and not for *things*. Remember, as each robbery came and went, he got more sloppy. His subconscious was begging for a way out. Pleading to be caught. A longing for stability. Regulation. Peace.

Hayes reacts immediately to my musings. "I don't even have to think about that one. Yes. That is why I kept driving down to Santa Clarita. That's why I kept traveling down Highway 33. That is why I robbed the same bank twice! I knew what I was doing was wrong."

So even if it was jail, it was three meals a day, it was regulated, and it would quiet down the noise in his head and the spinning top that had become his life. Jail was relief.

And that is how a $19-million dollar lottery winner was arrested - and facing 80 years in prison at trial.

Approximately six months later, the state of California offered an open-ended plea deal, which he and his public defender accepted. He was sentenced to 33 months in prison and ordered to pay $39,424 in restitution to the banks he had robbed. The 33 months surprised even Hayes, but his prior criminal record was non-existent and he did have a record of charitable donations as well, both of which were conveyed prevalently in court. He was encouraged by his lawyer to lean into the drug addiction part of the story as well.

Hayes recollects those moments with a mix of pride and maybe a little shame. "I was featured on America's Most Wanted three times and at one point, I was #10 on the Ten Most Wanted list. I had no idea about the implications of getting caught. I thought I would go down in gunfire with the cops. I thought it was a victimless crime. But it's not. One teller, I really scared her, and I will carry that with me forever," he says through tears. "I don't know what happened to her but I realize that fear could ripple through all of her life in so many ways and affect so many people and relationships in her life. And this is going to follow me forever and to my next life. It's branded on my soul. It's something I have to live with. And it also inspires me to get the message out to people not to do this. I wish I would have a better sense of financial obligations. I over-gave, I over-spent. I think it's so important to get the word out to future winners—what's good and what's bad."

* * *

But it wasn't quite over for him yet. Hayes went to the Federal Correctional Institution at Terminal Island in San Pedro, CA. He immediately found himself detoxing off his heroin habit. He was trembling, very sick, had a hard time walking, and was very scared. His initial bunk was a 2-man cell on the 7th floor, but he suddenly woke up in the psych unit on the 8th floor in a 5-man cell, with medical monitors attached all over his body. He had no idea how much time had passed between the 7th and 8th floor and no memory of how he got there.

"They told me I had a grand mal seizure and that I was taken to the hospital and they revived me. I was detoxing so badly that I guess I pretty much died. So, my start in prison was rough. I was in that 8th-floor observation unit for about a month and I started feeling normal again—eating food, getting my head straight, and then they came and moved me out of the med unit to the 9th floor. They called it gladiator school. It was where the murderers and the bank robbers were. My first cellmate was the nicest guy ever. Russian. I forget his name. But he had killed multiple people in the Russian mafia. Nicest killer I met in prison! People didn't mess with me because I was his cellmate."

Hayes is on a roll now. "You have to put on your game face there, though. You lock eyes with the wrong person and you could get killed. There's two types of prisoners: predators and prey. I was neither. I just couldn't comply with prison politics. I ended up in solitary a lot. I probably didn't go outside for two years and I got two showers a week. They do allow you to receive paperback books, though, so I read nothing but psychology and history books. Lots of religious books, Hinduism, Islam, and others. I studied the whole time I was there and I learned a lot. I actually found some happiness in solitary. I realized what I was missing. The happiest place that I was missing was right between my ears. I rebuilt myself. That's what prison did to me and it probably saved my life."

The days, weeks, and months marched on and, like nearly all prisoners, Hayes had plenty of time to think and assess. To dream about his day of release. To envision someone waiting for him when they unlocked the gates. But even that didn't play out exactly the way he had dreamed.

"The cruel joke is that part of my life is gone forever. The worst year of my life was the year I got out of prison. Stephanie kind of broke my heart. She decided she didn't want to stick by me and we separated when I went to prison. I have different theories about why she did this. It makes me sad that when I did need her, she wasn't there. I wouldn't ever in a million years abandon her like that. I don't hate her, but it sure made life tough on me when I got out. But maybe it's better that nobody helps you, because you learn to help yourself.

"We had a great marriage until I became a bank robber," he adds with uproarious laughter. "She's a very good person."

Yin and Yang just kept smacking Hayes around. He was released on April 1, 2020, and he doesn't hesitate to note the irony of being released on April Fools Day. His newfound freedom found him at his biological mother's bedside. She was dying of Cancer and had COVID. Her family wanted her to remain at home and not in a hospital with COVID restrictions so they could be with her and see her.

"My probation was so strict. The first time I got a violation my mom was sick; she lasted 24 days. I sat by her side every day. I kinda went off the deep end and smoked some pot. They let it slide that time, but three months later I took a urine test and failed that, so I went back to prison for three months, right back in the same cell. I got out for the second time and I got into some problems and I couldn't find a job again. I had nowhere to live. They let me out only because I agreed to go to rehab. I know guys in prison who won't leave! They decide to do the whole term because probation can be so tough that it's easier for the guy to just stay in. I'd see guys leave and they'd come right back."

Hayes would spend another two years either in prison for short stints (two total) or on probation. On July 7, 2022, he was officially taken off probation. A free man. He believes his years spent in prison saved his life, educated him, and re-connected him with faith.

"My faith got me out of a life sentence for bank robbery. The first thing you need to do is have faith. If you don't believe in it, make yourself believe. I'm not so much religious, I don't go to church. But I believe in faith. I believe in Jesus. He was not of this Earth. I believe what the Bible said was true. Maybe some stuff got lost in translation. God, Allah, Buddha, whatever, the philosophy I use is supreme intelligence. I had lost faith when I was in Catholic high school and I can't tell you when it happened but for a while, I did stop believing there was a god. When I got into a really big pickle after being arrested for those bank robberies, I prayed. I prayed and said 'god, if you are really there I want you to let me know. Are you real?' He didn't appear right there but three weeks later he answered me."

Hayes declines to expand on what happened three weeks later but is clearly adept at self-promotion. He promises to reveal just how he was answered in his autobiography.

"I know there's people who need help. Maybe my story will help them make a decision that's the opposite of what I did. I have to be careful because my actions can influence someone. But now my purpose is to get my story out there as accurately as I can. I understand now that I'm responsible for every ripple when I throw a stone. God has spared me because he wants me to get the message out."

Typical of the entire interview, Hayes careens back and forth from the serious to the humorous. Yin and yang. "I'm really god's court jester," he laughs loudly. "I think my story could help someone out there on the fence and thinking about doing something stupid."

Life today is more simple for James Hayes. He was invited by a childhood neighbor and friend to get out of California and go across the country to a small town in Virginia, where he resides today. He's working on his aforementioned book and there's also a documentary about his life that recently wrapped, backed by a real production company. He hopes it will be picked up by one of the major streaming services.

In the meantime, he's looking into working in real estate or, no surprise, the car business; the love of fast cars remains close to his heart. He also met someone.

"Best girl I've ever met. I tell her all my flaws. She and her daughter love me to death. It was a big piece of my life missing that I never thought I'd get back again. I think she's an angel right from heaven," he says in tears again. "I just want to pay bills, I don't want a Lamborghini. I just want a simple life. I never imagined in a million years I'd be where I am. I can't tell you how happy this girl makes me. Virginia has been a fresh start and I have a woman who loves me and I'm so grateful. I appreciate every little thing so much. I'm sitting here looking at leaves and birds outside and it's beautiful."

CHAPTER FOUR
Who Plays

Many people claim that the lottery is a poor man's tax. The low-income, downtrodden, and desperate among usspending the most. But do we actually know that? Is it even knowable?

Smarter people than me have asked this question for years. In fact, there are three published studies that sought to discover exactly who plays the lottery: one on the National Library of Medicine website, another published out of Ohio State University, and a third based on some research at the Massachusetts Institute of Technology (MIT). Combined, they provide a glimpse into some lottery demographics as well as saving and spending trends. If you like terms such as "negative binomial regression analysis," then by all means, proceed to the mind-melting math in these incredibly detailed studies that I am referencing! But there will be no mind-melting in this chapter, just a basic paraphrasing of what these studies found. This chapter is the plain English translation of the study; celebrate it as a selfless effort to keep you awake and (hopefully) interested.

The first study, published by the National Library of Medicine in late 2011, is titled *Gambling on the Lottery:*

Sociodemographic Correlates Across the Lifespan[37]. When I start my punk-rock band, "sociodemographic correlates across the lifespan" will be the title of the first song on the album. This study was funded by grants from the National Institute on Mental Health and the National Institute on Alcohol Abuse and Alcoholism. It was done via two telephone surveys conducted in the United States where gambling was the main topic.

The target survey participants were:

a) adults aged 18 years and older (2,631 participants, from 1999 to 2000)

b) people aged 14 – 21 years old (2,274 participants, from 2005 to 2007)

Questions and methods were largely the same in both groups surveyed and the resulting data were combined into a single set of data. This data set assessed gambling habits and problem-gambling signals pertaining only to the lottery, given that the lottery is the largest form of gambling in the U.S.A. The report also combines data and learnings from other prior studies into its summarization.

The report found that the frequency of gambling and spending on the lottery jumped significantly from mid-adolescence to age 18, which is the legal age to play state lotteries in the majority of the U.S. Surprise! Kids in their late teens aren't always responsible with their money! Spending on the lottery continued to increase into a person's 30s and at that point, their spending stabilized and largely stayed the

---

[37] Barnes GM, Welte JW, Tidwell MC, Hoffman JH. Gambling on the lottery: sociodemographic correlates across the lifespan. J Gambl Stud. 2011 Dec;27(4):575-86. doi: 10.1007/s10899-010-9228-7. PMID: 21132521; PMCID: PMC4103646.

same all the way through their 60s. That's four decades where the people polled said they spent the same amount on the lottery year after year. It wasn't until age 70 and up that a person's spending on the lottery started to see a decrease, which is not surprising, as income from work has usually stopped and disposable cash has likely dwindled a bit. Or perhaps 70 years old is the magical age where people (finally) realize that money, while nice to have, isn't the answer to all of their problems.

You may have noticed a six-year difference between the adult survey and the teen survey. To address this, the report states that key data was considered among the 18 to 21-year-old groups in each of the surveys to determine any differences. For example, the number of days 18 to 21-year-olds gambled in the past year was 53 times in the adult survey and 55 times in the teen survey. Among lottery players only, the 18 to 21-year-olds in the adult survey averaged 26.8 days playing the lottery in the past year and the figure for 18 to 21-year-olds in the teen survey was 22.9 days. The report points out that "these are not meaningful differences; and thus, there is no evidence of a chronological gambling trend in the time between the two surveys."

Both age group surveys included questions on how often in the past 12 months the respondent participated in fifteen types of lottery games, including instant scratch tickets, daily numbers, or lotto games. The analyses also included gender, race and ethnicity, and whether the lottery was legal in the state where the survey-taker lived.

Socioeconomic status, average years of education, and prestige scores for occupations were also considered and included. For the adult-only survey, respondents were asked directly. For the teen survey, respondents were asked about the average years of their parent's education and occupation.

Neighborhood disadvantage also factored into the survey,

based on data from the respondent's area census results. In simple terms, this means that the survey factored in the following:

- the percentage of households on public assistance
- the percentage of households headed by a female
- the percentage of adults unemployed
- the percentage of persons in poverty

OK, that was all a mouthful. Let's get to the results of this self-reported, surveyed data.

When looking at gender, self-described males reported lottery participation for 18.3 days in the past year, whereas self-described females reported 11.7 days for the same time period—that's a 63% difference in frequency.

When looking at age, 14% of people aged 14 to 15 played a lottery in the past year, and 16% of 16 to 17 year-olds said the same. The percentage for young adults aged 18 to 21 is where that number jumps to 50%. This jump from 14% and 16% up to 50% makes perfect sense as it becomes much easier to gamble on the lottery at the legal age of 18.

The 22 to 39 age group is where the percentage of gamblers reached its apex. In this age group, 70–71% of the respondents report that they played a lottery game in the prior 12 months. It starts to trail down a bit after that with approximately 66% of adults in their forties, fifties, and sixties reporting that they gambled on the lottery in the past year. As mentioned before, the percentage takes a solid drop down to 45% for people 70 and older.

When looking at racial and ethnic groups, the study says that non-Hispanic white people and Native Americans had the highest rates of gambling on the lottery, at 51% for each group. With regard to "mean levels of gambling on the lottery," the report states that African Americans and Native

Americans had the highest average frequency, at 20.6 days and 25 days in the past year, respectively. Asians had the lowest mean levels of lottery play, averaging 8.1 days.

The economic status of the survey participants also offered some interesting data. Those in the lowest fifth of earnings had the highest rate of lottery gambling (at 61%) and the highest mean amount of days playing the lottery (at 26.1 days in the past year). Interestingly, the top three groups of economic earners were all very similar; 42% to 43% of the three groups gambled on the lottery and played an average of 10 days in the past year. Neighborhood economical status, called "neighborhood disadvantage" in the survey, showed that survey-takers who lived in an area with the highest neighborhood disadvantage had the highest number of days gambling on the lottery, at 19.6 in the past 12 months.

The two most significant factors in the analysis appear to be the individuals' economic status and the neighborhood disadvantage (the latter is based on census data).

In the analysis of economic variables, including individual economic status and neighborhood disadvantage, Black and Hispanic groups were found to not be statistically much different from the white reference group in terms of the number of days gambled on the lottery. The study adds, however, that Native Americans "remained significantly more likely to gamble on the lottery in spite of all of the other sociodemographic factors considered and in spite of a fairly small number of Native Americans in the sample."

Lower economic status in this study is clearly linked to frequent gambling on the lottery among adults. Combining the survey data of youths and adults, the lowest economic group had the highest percentage of gambling on the lottery and the highest average mean in terms of number of days playing the lottery. Curiously, these two deltas went away when neighborhood disadvantage was added into the mix.

The report states that "Neighborhood disadvantage is correlated with low socioeconomic status and minority race/ethnicity, yet it may also represent a broader ecological factor – a cultural milieu where lotteries are easily available and an environment favorably inclined to gambling on the lottery."

The ending summary of this study states this:

It is clear that lottery play is a popular form of entertainment among adults with a majority of those in their twenties through sixties reporting that they had gambled on the lottery in the past year…on the other hand, increased levels of lottery play are linked with certain subgroups in the U.S. population – males, Blacks, Native Americans, and those who live in disadvantaged neighborhoods. The present findings do not resolve the debate about lotteries in the U.S., but they do help to inform the discussion.

The second report is authored by researcher Jay Zagorsky, whom you met in the first chapter. While employed as a Research Scientist at Ohio State University's Center for Human Resource Research in 2012, he authored a fascinating study[38] about financial inheritances, including lottery winnings. His aim was to understand how people use their money after acquiring large sums of cash. Here is the text of our conversation, slightly edited for clarity:

Q: Do people who win the lottery blow it more than people who inherit money from family?

A: There are no academic studies that I know of which have a true comparison of the two. But the world is big and

---

[38] https://news.osu.edu/most-americans-save-only-about-half-of-their-inheritances-study-finds---ohio-state-research-and-innovation-communications/

there's a lot of knowledge out there. Just because I read a lot and look for a lot doesn't necessarily mean that I covered everything. Sometimes there are stones that I don't know about.

Q: That's fair. Did you pick up any signals in your study between the two, though?

A: People do a lot of something called mental accounting, where we put money into various buckets in our heads. And sometimes we even do it physically. Some people physically put money into different and specific bank accounts. I know somebody who had four different checking accounts. Each having its own purpose. And one aspect of behavioral economics is that when people earn money, it's treated differently. For example, you sell books and you get a royalty check. You feel you've done something for that money, and you tend to spend that very differently than money that just sort of drops down from the heavens. And when gifts come down, they're really treated very differently.

Q: Meaning that people who inherit money from a loved one may be more careful than people who win money in the lottery?

A: I'd contend that people tend not to be as cautious with lottery money. People basically treat lottery winnings as fun money. Free money. With free money, it's like, okay, we can go drinking, we can go on vacations, we can just do everything, but we don't necessarily save it. Now, there are some people who don't approach it in this manner. And I think that's why you're finding a few people who find that the lottery was wonderful and they were very responsible with it. But for the vast majority of people, it's free money. They didn't actually earn it, it just came accidentally. And because it came accidentally, they don't have to think very hard when they're spending it, they have a good time.

Q: Right. So tell me a little about the study you did in 2012.
A: For me, the real key is table six in that study. Table six tells us if they basically saved any money from their inheritance.

Table 6 Percent of inheritors who saved by inheritance amount (in 2009 $)

Amount inherited	Overall among inheritors	$1 to $999	$1,000 to $4,999	$5,000 to $9,999	$10,000 to $49,999	$50,000 to $99,999	$100,000 and above	No inheritance
Negative savings	33.9%	39.8%	36.8%	34.2%	29.5%	29.5%	18.2%	39.1%
Zero savings	1.0%	1.8%	0.8%	1.3%	0.5%	0.6%	0.5%	4.0%
Positive savings	65.1%	58.5%	62.5%	64.5%	69.9%	69.9%	81.3%	56.9%
Number observations	8,180	2,174	2,272	1,043	1,932	352	407	106,608

Results are weighted to represent all U.S. young baby boomers

Table 6, "Do People Save or Spend Their Inheritances? Understanding What Happens to Inherited Wealth"
Author: Jay Zagorsky

A (continued): You can read exactly how we calculate the wealth in the paper. But we knew their wealth at a particular point in time. We know they inherited some money, because they reported it to me. They got a windfall, small, medium, or large. So I knew their wealth at one point, and then I knew it at a particular point later on in time.

Q: And what does wealth include in your study?
A: Wealth includes things like cash, cars, and homes. Things. So if I suddenly was given or won a million dollars and I went out and bought a house with it, then my savings went up by a million, because the house is an asset. I bought a car or some jewelry, or an RV. All that would still be captured as savings. Pretty straightforward. So the top line [in the above Table 6] is people with negative savings, their assets minus the liabilities. Negative savings means they

actually went down after getting an inheritance. To me, it's kind of amazing that among everybody in the study, about a third actually saw their wealth go down. And all you have to do is just go buy diamonds or something.

Q: Gosh. What did they do with it?

A: I don't know. It can't be good if you're going to go out and just piss it all away. That's your net worth!

Q: I see that the percentage goes down as the money increases. Do you think that it's because it might be harder to spend more money or do you think there's something sociological going on there?

A: I can't tell you. But as you get more and more money, it is tougher and tougher to spend quickly. This is a relatively short time frame that I'm looking at here. This study was published ten years ago, so I can't tell you exactly the time frame I measured, but … I was looking at something like a year-and-a-half or two years. But if someone gives you—or if you win—$200,000, it's tough to blow it all in just one year.

Q: The negative savings line is sobering. Basically, just under one-third of people who win or inherit money don't just blow it all, they blow it all and *then some*!

A: And it's not only that line, but the zero savings line is also there. So adding the negative savings line and the zero savings line together, more than one-third showed nothing in their detailed net worth. And this wasn't a small sample, it was 8,000 people!

Q: What other notable patterns did you pick up from your study, particularly in Table 6?

A: It's a pretty straightforward pattern, this downward slope. But the slope is pretty high. When I conducted the research, I was expecting that most people would have positive savings and only a few outliers wouldn't, but no.

Q: Do you think anything has changed in the last ten years? If you were to revisit all this, do you think there's anything that would be different?

A: Until I actually do a follow-up study, I can't definitively say, of course. To be a betting man right now, though, no, I don't. The reason I haven't done another study is that I think the results are the same. If I do one every ten years, I really doubt it looks any different. People, I believe, are people. We're talking about a deep-seated sort of psychological phenomena, individuals who got free money, who are clearly going to spend a lot of it. A large amount of whom will have nothing to show for it. It is what it is.

Q: Outside of your story, have you witnessed this in your own life, where someone won or inherited money and just blew it all?

A: I used to play a lot of basketball before COVID. Organized leagues, things like that. They were fairly expensive with refs, scorekeepers, and all. We had a guy who was, I would say, relatively cheap, and one day the captain convinced everyone to go for a beer down the street. And this guy got there first and he was bored so he played Keno. The rest of us all walked in a little later and the guy is jumping up and down because he just won a lot of money. Before this he was incredibly cheap, but now he was like, "Food's on me! Drinks on me! Whatever you want!" I was like, what just happened? He was actually in deep debt to the coach! But by the end of the night, the guy was broke again. He spent his entire casino winnings that night.

Q: Wait. How much did he win??

I think it was like $600. Somewhere in that range. If you win more than $600, you can't get paid off at the bar, and he did. And then it was gone! He bought rounds of drinks and burgers for everybody and their brother. And I was like, well, thanks for the beer, but more than that, thanks for the story. But once again, he didn't feel that he'd earned it. He was kind of bored. And he threw a couple of bucks down from Keno, he won and he had nothing to show for it afterward.

Q: Did he at least pay off the debts to the coach and the guys who floated him?
A: He did pay off his debt to the coach, and that's good.

Q: So do you play the lottery?
A: I play the lottery whenever the Powerball or Mega Millions gets above $500 million or so. I actually had this conversation about 45 minutes before I talked to you, the person said he also played once the number got relatively high. And he and I both agreed that two $2 bet is worth 10 minutes of daydreaming. You got 10 minutes of entertainment.

Q: Yeah, that's a small price to pay for a good, fun conversation about what you would do with it. Back to inheritances in general and financial responsibility. It seems our kids, young people, are not taught anything in high school or even grade school about being smart with money. Should they be? Should there be some kind of mandate to do that?
A: It depends on which state you're living in. There's been a fair amount of academic work that suggests that classes for 15 or 16-year-olds about credit card debt have no impact on their future financial life, or it has only an extremely muted impact. But there are a number of states that do try to make

sure the kids are a little bit educated about money.

Q: But isn't muted impact or tiny impact better than nothing? Isn't it better than just pushing these kids into the world with no education about financial responsibility and then having them suddenly be $30,000 in debt on a credit card?

A: In my mind, the reason it doesn't work is you're educating people who've not actually had jobs. They've not dealt with money on their own before. So teaching someone about a credit card who can't actually get one for another 5 or 6 years? We tend to lose the lessons. It's much more salient if you're giving a credit card lesson as it's happening. So they can see what's happening if they don't pay it. They can see what's going on. But they don't see anything. I've never written a paper on it, but I've looked at a lot of data.

Q: Since this book is more lottery-focused than inheritance-focused, do you think that state lottery commissions should mandate or require some kind of financial training for lottery winners?

A: First, I do not believe states should mandate financial education in order to pick up your check. I believe a lot of this is personal responsibility. Second, there are a fair number of TV shows, radio shows, and things like that where you see the story of someone who won a whole bunch of money, they take it all upfront, and it ends up being a disaster. I say if you do win a lottery, always, always take the extended payout. And even if I mandate a course to you and you've won $500 million, no two-hour course is going to prepare you for that. Nobody can really explain to you what it's like to suddenly get a check for $500 million. Get the extended payouts and after the first one or two, you'll figure out how to actually run your life.

* * *

Q: I think the theory with taking it all upfront is that you can probably do better in the long run if you invest it wisely.

A: That is completely true. The annuities are based on the current interest rates. Current interest rates are relatively low, so the annuity is not paying off very much. If you invest in the stock market, you're going to earn a couple of percent more. But I feel like if you double your winnings in size, you're not talking about $500 million, now you're talking about $1 billion. Why do you need a billion?

Q: Just to be able to log in to online banking and see it!

A: Okay, that's great. But if $500 million doesn't change your life, I'm not sure a billion is going to change your life. It is more likely going to destroy your life. Back to my study, it's about what you keep afterward. 35% of people actually end up with negative savings, which means they're not even buying homes or cars, or jewelry. They're just spending it with nothing to show for it.

The third report[39], published in 2011 at M.I.T., is titled *The Ticket To Easy Street? The Financial Consequences Of Winning The Lottery.* In a nutshell, this research seeks to answer if cash windfalls given to financially distressed people are just a temporary solution to inevitable bankruptcy, or if that cash truly puts a struggling person on the path to stability. It complements Jay Zagorsky's research in that we'll get a more

[39] Scott Hankins, Mark Hoekstra, Paige Marta Skiba; The Ticket to Easy Street? The Financial Consequences of Winning the Lottery. *The Review of Economics and Statistics* 2011; 93 (3): 961–969. doi: https://doi.org/10.1162/REST_a_00114

specific glimpse into the mentality of large cash acquisition events and people's tendencies. Do they just spend it all right away on frivolous goods that aren't tied to net worth as 35% of Zagorsky's subjects did? Zagorsky also referenced "mental accounting". The M.I.T. research also digs into how people treat cash when they have a free-money mentality. Do they purchase luxury goods and then become entrenched in that lifestyle, putting themselves into even deeper debt? Do they even have the knowledge to handle large amounts of cash? The report also cites other surveys that have "consistently shown that U.S. adults have relatively low levels of financial literacy." This is not a shock. Zagorsky's research also complements that notion.

Specifically, the M.I.T. researchers looked at a set of winners of the Florida Lottery and compared them to bankruptcy records. The information on the lottery winners was obtained from the Florida Lottery and included every winner of the Fantasy 5 game from April 29, 1993, through November 27, 2002.

They also compared lottery winners of amounts from $50,000 to $150,000 to people who won less than $10,000. They assume that winning the lottery has nothing to do with the winner's "underlying propensity for bankruptcy," also making clear they found no differences in demographics or bankruptcy rates of large-cash winners or small-cash winners in the years prior to winning the lottery.

So, what *did* they find?

They found that giving people $50,000 to $150,000 doesn't prevent future bankruptcy, it only postpones it. And while recipients were 50% less likely to file for bankruptcy immediately after receiving the cash windfall, they were more likely to file for bankruptcy three to five years later. There was no difference in larger cash amounts or smaller cash amounts, according to bankruptcy petitions. Simply put, a person in dire need of financial assistance won between $50,000 and $150,000 and could have paid off some, if not all, of their debt and possibly even added assets to their net worth. They did neither. They didn't really buy anything that helped their net worth. Ouch.

There were no statistical differences between these two groups' bankruptcy rates prior to winning. There were no differences in the assets, debts, incomes, or expenditures of those winners who *did* file bankruptcy prior to winning the lottery.

In more closely examining the bankruptcy filings, the report shows that the rates of bankruptcy aren't different, but those winners of amounts from $25,000 to $150,000 who went on to file for bankruptcy later did so with virtually the same amount of net assets and debt. The bankruptcy records showed little evidence that large winners filed for bankruptcy because of debt incurred from a house purchase. There is also a homestead exemption in Florida bankruptcy law, which wasn't a factor either, in other words, nobody was really trying to game the system in that way.

The findings lock in two major takeaways. First, in terms of large vs. small-cash winnings, people still filed for bankruptcy at the same rate. Second, the long-term positive impact of winning the lottery for people who are in dire need of cash is pretty much non-existent.

This is sobering.

And sad.

Combining these three reports provides a glimpse into who plays the lottery, what typically happens to the money, and a person's financial standing afterward. It is by no means a definitive picture, but the sample sizes are most certainly large enough to paint a broad-strokes picture. According to these findings, the most likely lottery player is an African-

American or Native-American male in his 20s or 30s, living in a disadvantaged neighborhood with lower earnings. Of those lucky enough to win money in a lottery, 35% of them will have either no savings or negative savings from their winnings within 18 to 24 months. While it may help them stave off bankruptcy temporarily, it doesn't prevent it, it just delays it.

Poor-man's tax, indeed.

CHAPTER FIVE

Dawn Nettles

"I'm at war with the lottery." This is one of the first things that Dawn Nettles tells me when I interview her.

The 70-year-old from the Dallas suburb of Garland, Texas, owns and operates a website called the Lotto Report (lottoreport.com). At first glance, you may believe you've hopped in a time machine and are trapped in a pixellated alternate online Geocities universe. She makes no apologies for it and does not claim to be anywhere close to web savvy.

The Lotto Report provides information on the Texas lottery. While there are posts like up-to-date winning numbers, it's apparent that the primary purpose of the website is to throw serious shade at the state-run Texas Lottery Commission. There is a significant amount of accusations and criticism of the commission to be found there. It contains updates on lawsuits and court decisions pertaining to lotteries in Texas, some of which she initiated and/or is involved in. She pulls no punches in her efforts to bring transparency and fairness to a system she feels is very much rigged in favor of the state. And she's got the bruises to prove it. As a very vocal advocate for the rights of lottery players in Texas, she has helped to expose several cases of perceived corruption within the commission and she has no plans to slow down.

"They don't want you talking to me," she says, matter-of-factly, with her slight Texas drawl. "The lottery commission here pretends to care about education, but all they're doing is trying to screw people out of their money. There is no consumer protection whatsoever. They make it impossible to win. I can't speak for lotteries outside of Texas, but lotteries here cheat players, and they don't pay them their rightful amount of money even if they do win. But here's the thing—it's really the poor folks who lose, and many of them don't know the rules. Even some lawyers don't know the rules. I have lawyers and financial advisors calling me when they have questions. Many lawyers don't think to question the validity of what they've been told by the lotteries in terms of their client's winnings."

She is so well known that when Texas citizens and winners have a problem, they often reach out to her. She says the lottery commission knows her well and she is a proud member of many of their shit lists. She defiantly says, "In Texas, the lottery knows better now because of me. People reach out to me. They know me. Every time there's a problem, I get a call. I'm on a lot of people's shit list at the state commission."

It's safe to say that Dawn Nettles is an unchained, bonafide lottery watchdog.

"I didn't even know the lottery existed when I was young," she says. "The closest thing I did as a little kid would be spending summers with my grandmother in Wichita Falls; we would go to the Catholic church to play bingo with my grandma. Growing up, I loved playing cards, too, but had no awareness of the lottery. Later on, I discovered casinos, yeah, Las Vegas and all...I do like a good game. I'm not an addictive gambler, and I always lose. And that's what we need to make more people aware of. Losing."

* * *

In 1992, Nettles worked in the magazine business focused on real estate and relocation. One day while at a country club, a group of builders mentioned that there was a large jackpot in that night's lottery. Knowing she was a publisher, they encouraged her to start producing a periodical related to lotteries. Over a short time, she found it intriguing enough to combine her knowledge of publishing with her growing interest in lottery games, and the Lotto Report was born. In 1992, with online publishing virtually non-existent, the Lotto Report was printed (on paper!) bi-weekly and sold at convenience stores and the like.

"It was kind of like the horse-racing forms," Nettles explains, "you get one and you go to a restaurant or a bar and figure out which horse you wanted to bet on. It was like that, except with lottery numbers—what balls have been dropped the most, what's the trends, what games are hot, what's not, and that sort of stuff. I published it every week. First thing people said to me was 'people aren't gonna buy that. People would rather spend their money on lottery tickets than a lottery report.' But people bought it. It sold about as much as I wanted it to sell."

That was her first foray into the inner workings of the Texas Lottery Commission, but far from her last.

"In 1996, the Texas Lottery decided that the sales weren't enough on their premier Lotto Texas game, so they decided they would make some changes to the rules. They changed from a 20 to a 25-year payout, and I guess I was pretty dumb because I didn't understand it and thought it was weird. But people kept calling me because I published the Lotto Report and were saying that the Commission was screwing the people big-time with that. And I didn't really understand it until 1998, when they decided to make another rule change, this time expanding the pick-six to 54 numbers instead of 50 numbers. Well, I knew that might hurt my little business because it would change the odds so much."

With her publication and voice growing as a consumer-friendly authority, Dawn Nettles publicly opposed this change. The Texas Lottery Commission wasn't intimidated by this one woman and pushed forward on the change, but they did inform Nettles about a way for citizens to register a comment with a federal agency. This feature allows citizens to be heard when a proposed rule or regulation is under consideration. Nettles believed she had a way to cut off this proposed change at the pass. All she had to do was submit a Public Comment.

"And so I did," she said, "and they didn't expect that. I got around 3,000 signatures opposing the rule and ... I went to a commission meeting, and they ended up deciding to withdraw the change! And I thought, 'wow, look at that, it worked!' But then a reporter at the Dallas Morning News pulled me aside and said, 'Hey Dawn, don't celebrate too much; they're just going to propose another rule and make a couple of changes. You haven't really done anything.'"

Perhaps that was true, but Nettles had busted through another wall.

As predicted by the reporter, the Texas Lottery Commission did indeed come back to the table with a similar set of proposed changes to the game. This time, the commission worked with GTech[40] to petition all the retailers and get their *own* papers signed.

* * *

---

[40] At the time, GTech was a technology company based in Providence, Rhode Island, United States, focused on the lottery and gaming. It exists today as International Game Technology (IGT) through several name changes, mergers, and acquisitions over the years. It is now a multi-billion dollar corporation focused on lottery and gaming technology.

Nettles goes on, "So I obtained copies of the petitions, and I hired forensic experts to look at the handwriting. They said it looked like the same 3 or 4 people writing everything. I got a second forensic expert to look at it, and they had the same conclusion."

With Nettles pursuits with forensic experts pseudoscientific, the changes to the game were approved anyway by the Texas Lottery Commission, despite Nettles's contention that some of the petitions may have been fraudulent.

Nettles was beside herself. "Then it became a war. I exposed GTech; they actually relocated the leader of GTech at the time. So that's how it all started in 1998," she laughs. "The press called me 'the watchdog of the Texas lottery.' That's how I discovered players are getting cheated.

"Players are the poor folks, for the most part. Let's talk about scratch tickets. They buy a lot of them and they only scratch to expose the barcode, then just hand them all to the clerk to scan to see which ones are winners. If there's a winning ticket for $100, a clerk will tell the customer they won $10, and then the clerk just pockets the rest. These customers are easy targets. And these clerks change jobs, store to store to store. And they make a whole lot of money off lottery players."

You may be tempted to not have a shred of sympathy for anyone, rich or poor, who does not properly scratch off their card. Further lack of sympathy may be in order when the player then hands that ticket to a store clerk and just believes the news from the clerk that it's not a winner. But the old adage of walking a mile in someone else's shoes applies here. A desperate person's story is often very much their own story and is rarely known, comprehended or understood by bystanders. This applies to both player and clerk. This is a much bigger issue than the Texas Lottery Commission or

Dawn Nettles.

Nettles, though, isn't just a commission watchdog; she is also a staunch consumer advocate.

"I had a lottery winner out of San Antonio and honestly he played too many scratch tickets. We were going down for a lottery commission meeting in Austin, and I asked him to bring me a bunch of unscratched tickets. We found out how much money was won on each and a few of us went to stores to see what the clerks would say when he handed them a ticket that we all knew was a winner." She explains that one person would pretend to be the player and the others would shop and act as if they didn't know each other.

"We went to four or five stores and all of the clerks were honest. That was good. Then we went to another store, and the clerk stuck the first ticket in the machine, tore it in half, and threw it away. Then the same with the second one. Then the third one…and on and on. After he scanned all of them, he said, 'sorry, they're all losers.' We started moving a little closer, and the clerk saw us coming, staring at him, and then suddenly changed his tune and said, 'oh wait—they're all winners!'"

Nettles says she brought this story to the Texas Lottery Commission. "We went to the commission meeting and gave live testimony. They didn't care or do anything about it."

Take a moment and look at the scratch ticket below. This is a close-up of a Texas Lottery game released on September 2, 2014, called Fun 5's. Each ticket had five sections and each of the five sections was its own separate sub-game. Below was one of the five sub-games. Please read it carefully.

* * *

Here are those directions again for the same sub-game, blown up a little larger:

In reading the instructions and looking at the game, which of the following two scenarios do you believe to be true based on the directions?

1) This sub-game offers a <u>single</u> chance to win: get three 5 symbols in a row, and you win. To see how much you won, scratch off the prize area, then scratch the 5X box to see if your prize is multiplied times five.

2) This sub-game offers <u>two</u> ways to win. Even if you don't get the three 5 symbols in a row, you still win by seeing a money bag in the 5X box and you scratch the prize area to see your winning amount.

Regardless of your opinion about the above scenario, the instructions on the ticket should probably be more precise. This level of ambiguity may not be malicious or intended, but it can be argued that it's unclear. A person reading these instructions may believe they have won when they have not. And many believed that they had won. Nettles contends this is particularly unfair to certain groups of people or people who don't speak fluent American English. She believes that the Texas Lottery makes these instructions purposefully vague and labels these types of tickets as "deceptive" or "trick" tickets.

So here's the answer. In order to win, you must meet both criteria!

"The Fun 5's game was used in multiple states," she explains. "The same ticket with the exact language, and when players uncovered the special symbol, they thought they had won five times the amount. They did not have to win the tic-tac-toe portion. Texas has admitted to *not* changing the instructions after adding the special symbol to non-winning tickets and then purposely put the special symbols on non-winning tickets because of store clerks pin-pricking them and taking the winning tickets. But they failed to change the instructions on how to win."

Nettles is clearly frustrated by these "trick tickets" and further supports her position by adding, "Why in the hell is the unclaimed-prize fund so large? The Lottery puts out these trick tickets, these deceptive tickets, and players may just miss things. They think they lost, and they just throw them away. At first, I thought it was terminals," which she claims is another way the lottery comes out ahead. "Some terminals will say 'not a winner' for tickets that are winners. Nobody holds them accountable. They're selling games, and it's like a diet pill ad. You never lose weight. It's all fraudulent."

The question on the Fun 5's game is basically an and/or issue, and was a major point of a lawsuit initially filed by Nettles. "The day that ticket hit the stores in 2014, people started calling me left and right," she explains. "They were also calling the Texas Lottery and GTech. The Texas Lottery told people they basically didn't know how to read. They didn't want to pull the ticket. They just said, 'oh, this is just a Nettles thing.' I couldn't believe they would even continue to sell this. But they continued."

The Fun 5's lawsuit filed by Dawn Nettles was dismissed, and her appeal was overruled in 2017. Interestingly, the public filings[41] on this show that 1,200 other Fun 5's ticket purchasers in Texas sued GTech seeking damages in excess of $500 million, plus exemplary damages.

There is now a class action lawsuit that is still being litigated as of the writing of this book (ed. note: February 2023). Nettles claims that the Texas government has essentially turned their backs on it and claims that she has assisted many players in contacting elected officials about it. This is now close to a $1 billion lawsuit.

On a related note, while the Texas Lottery Commission was hesitant at first, sales of the Fun 5's scratch ticket were, in fact, discontinued on October 21, 2014, after about seven weeks on the market, which is significantly short for the lifespan of a scratch ticket. On her website, Nettles writes:

> No matter what the Texas Lottery will come up with to try to explain what they "meant" or "intended" for players to win…it was not conveyed and they MUST honor the face value and the written words found on their scratch tickets. Not doing so could/would be considered a crime by Texas statutes. There are too many tickets that pay prizes for a special character and is mixed in with other similar characters. Players notoriously fail to realize the ticket is a winner. Thousands of those prizes go unclaimed.

When I asked Nettles about players who call, she had a wealth of stories to share.

"I had a player call me from Dallas who had won on a scratch ticket. This person said he had won $1,507, but when we had it scanned at a store, the machine said he had won less than that. They determined it was a misprint, then all the tickets were pulled within a week. That player should collect the face value of the ticket, but it took a long time, and

---

[41] https://caselaw.findlaw.com/tx-court-of-appeals/1868538.html

eventually, the Texas Lottery Commission did instruct their vendor Sci Games to pay the player.

"One person who called me said they had bought a scratch ticket, and it was a $25,000 winner. They went home and hid the ticket under their mattress. The next day a friend of theirs came over, and the winner showed the guest the winning ticket. The next Monday morning, the winner was ready to take their ticket to Dallas to get their money and, looking under the mattress, found the ticket gone. The police were called, and once they knew that only one person had visited, they went immediately to that person's house, and she confessed she had stolen it. The thief had already given the ticket to another person who was actually en route to Dallas to get the money right then! So the Police notify the Texas Lottery Commission to hold that man when he gets there. The guy shows up in Dallas and fills out the claim form and ticket, and the official comes back, knowing this is an imposter with a stolen scratch ticket, and says the computers are down and that they would mail the check. Two years have passed and she still hasn't gotten her money! They say it's a property rights issue."

When sharing the details of one incident, Nettles's implied that a Texas Lottery Commission employee may have been receiving kickbacks from a preferred financial advisor.

"I had a financial institution call me. A big one. Gigantic. Very well known. This guy called me and said he's speaking out of turn and could lose his license, but felt he had to tell me about something that had happened at the Texas Lottery."

The employee had a lottery winner come to him with investments. The winner was unsatisfied with his first advisor, who had lost a great deal of money, and wanted to transfer the remaining investments over to a new advisor. The winner indicated that when he took his winning ticket to the Texas Lottery Commission office to collect the prize, one of the employees there handed him a card with a recommendation for a financial advisor.

"This could be a sign of kickbacks," Nettles says incredulously. "This guy at a huge financial institution was asking me to do something without ever mentioning his name. I looked into it and kept everything confidential like I said I would. I went to a commission meeting and testified and told them about it. The Commissioners immediately turned to the General Counsel and asked them to find out what was going on."

Nettles, a staunch consumer advocate and watchdog, was about to experience something she hadn't before.

"I thought, 'Holy cow, what have I stepped into?' They kept me back in a little room trying to get the info out of me, and I wouldn't tell them. I wouldn't tell them who came to me, and I wouldn't tell them what the financial institution was. Eventually, they walked me out the door. Next thing I knew, I received a call from Austin/Travis County District Attorney's office reminding me that my testimony is under oath."

The D.A.'s office pressured Nettles to reveal her source.

"They scared the shit out of me and intimidated me. I knew I needed a lawyer, and I got one. The lawyer said he would take care of it, so we called the financial guy who originally notified me. And the lawyer investigated and confirmed it all—I was telling the truth. My lawyer called the Austin D.A., and then the issue was dropped. Texas Lottery thought they had me for perjury! They told the United Press International that I was under investigation for perjury. The United Press International actually called to confirm. I told them my side, and the lottery told them their side. It was a big story."

Over the years, there have been additional legal disputes and controversies surrounding the commission's operations and management of the Texas Lottery, and Nettles has been at the forefront of many of them; allegations of fraud and misconduct by commission employees, accusations of poor management and a lack of transparency, lawsuits over access to public records, and the commission's general handling of specific games and promotions. And while the Texas Lottery has generated large sums of lottery revenue for public education, it also appears to be one of the more controversial state lottery commissions in the United States. Coincidence? Probably not. This 2014 article about Nettles ran in the New York Times on March 1, 2014.

Ms. Nettles is now questioning the constitutionality of the lottery's newest game: Texas Triple Chance. She said the game did not meet Texas' constitutional definition of a lottery because the state could benefit if no individual won the grand prize.

The commission's media relations director, Kelly Cripe, said the game was "designed in the same manner as other draw games offered by the Texas Lottery."

State Senator Bob Deuell, Republican of Greenville, is aiding an effort to look into the constitutionality of the game. His chief of staff, Don Forse, said that when the Legislature took up lottery issues, information from Ms. Nettles was always included in briefing packets.

"She sure is committed to a unique pet project," Mr. Forse said.

Ms. Nettles says she has specific goals to meet before she will consider ending The Lotto Report.

"I will retire from my work the day that the Texas Lottery or the Texas Legislature instructs the Texas Lottery to make good on cheated winners," she said.

* * *

Nettles does not charge for her efforts, but does make a small amount of money by producing a bi-weekly Pick3 Combinations report.

When asked what it's like to run a state lottery organization, what Texas does with the revenue from lottery sales, and thoughts on player protection and responsible gambling, a media relations official from the Texas Lottery Commission responded with appreciation for the inquiry but respectfully declined to participate by phone or by email.

When asked why she does it, Nettles answers quickly. "I'm stubborn. That's the short answer."

CHAPTER SIX

State Lottery Commissions

Regardless of the vitriol that Dawn Nettles seems to have for the authorities who run the lottery in Texas, the state lottery commissions in the United States all have their own structures and operational approaches. Most people seem to have no idea how a state lottery commission even works, what its purpose is, or how deeply intertwined they are with their respective state legislatures.

Enter Gregg Edgar. An affable, well-spoken guy who agreed to be interviewed for this book. The former Executive Director of the Arizona Lottery, he served the organization from 2016 until February of 2023.

He had this to say about people's lack of knowledge on how state lottery commissions work.

"Most people don't have any idea. I'll be honest, that's our fault because as an industry we don't talk about it well enough or discuss the impacts of it well enough. I'm a firm believer that when you look at gaming and the lottery in general that this is all a public policy decision, right? State and local leaders need to look at it from a standpoint of how much fun people want to have with the lottery. When you look at who lottery players are, these are folks, more often than not, who have disposable income and they view the lottery as pure entertainment. They feed their kids and put them to bed, and then they sit around the table and play the game. They scratch, and they dream big, and they spend what they can spend. There's a lot of people who enjoy that experience from an entertainment perspective."

Perhaps that's a view from the sunny side; rose-colored glasses and all. While the demographics don't exactly mirror that, Edgar's enthusiasm is, without question, palpable.

So, here's how it all works. There are state lottery commissions, state legislatures, there's the Multi-State Lottery Association (MUSL, pronounced mussel), and there's the North American Association of State & Provincial Lotteries (NAPSL, pronounced nap-sill). Then there's the YNWMMA, the You'll Never Win Mega Millions Association. OK, that last one might not exist, but if it did, it would potentially be the largest association in U.S. history. So, what gives? What on Earth do all these organizations do?

Gregg Edgar to the rescue.

"Let me take this apart from a couple of different ways. I'll start with step one—the United States. There are 48 different jurisdictions that are authorized to sell lottery. Note that I say jurisdictions, I don't say states because it includes the U.S. Virgin Islands, Puerto Rico, and Washington D.C. There are five states that do not have a lottery that's authorized by their legislature. I think what's key for you to understand as you do look at this, every single jurisdiction is different, with different laws and different regulatory burdens which are really reflective of the states that they sit in. Texas has a very different demographic from, say, New Jersey. The way gaming laws are structured in the United States, it's all done at a jurisdictional level. And then because that's done at the jurisdictional level, each lottery has a very different approach and a very different statutory scheme that they have to work under."

50 states minus 5 that don't play, and we get 45. Add the 3 territories that do, and we get 48.

Using an abacus for confirmation (hey, to be adept at writing and math is asking a lot of authors), the five states that don't offer lottery sales are Alabama, Alaska, Hawaii, Nevada, and Utah. You may think it odd that Nevada, U.S. gambling headquarters, doesn't have a state lottery system. But is it odd? Probably not. Not when there's already (what some consider) an embarrassing and dangerous over-abundance of gambling options already in place. Hawaii is probably just too chill for the lottery. Good for them! The three territories that don't offer lottery are American Samoa, Guam, and Northern Mariana Islands.

Edgar goes on to express, with maybe a combination of sarcasm and exasperation, what happens when all of these state lottery organizations gather.

"It's always hard to figure out what we can even do from a national perspective because in each jurisdiction there are many different rules."

Edgar continues, "Step two, you have MUSL, which consists of 38 state lottery jurisdictions. Those 38 jurisdictions have come together primarily for the running of multi-state draw games. MUSL operates Powerball, Lotto America, and a handful of smaller multi-state games. The 38 jurisdictions are responsible for the development, operations, planning, and rules that govern Powerball." The discerning reader will note that MUSL operates the Powerball game.

Edgar goes on to explain that in terms of MUSL operations, the 38 jurisdictions essentially have an ownership stake of sorts in MUSL. As the Executive Director of the Arizona lottery, he was a board member for MUSL. The Executive Directors of each state lottery commission (some may have different titles, so going forward we'll call them the leaders) make up the board of MUSL, and the percentage of ownership in MUSL is based on the percentage of sales each jurisdiction generates.

Wait a second. Why only 38? Where are the other 10, and why aren't those jurisdictions part of MUSL? The other 10 jurisdictions missing from MUSL make up the Mega Millions Consortium. Sadly, there are no cool abbreviations or initialisms for that organization. Just the Mega Millions Consortium. Perhaps they need a Creative Director. In looking at the list of those 10 jurisdictions, it's indeed noticeable that they tend to be states with larger populations, such as California, Washington, and Georgia.

"Yeah, it's a different group," Edgar explains, "I've actually not sat in their meetings, but the way they are structured is different than MUSL, relying more on the member jurisdictions for operations. There is a cross-sell agreement between the two entities that allows both products to be sold nationally.

"So, third step, you have the North American Association of State and Provincial Lotteries (NASPL), which is more like a traditional association, if you will. It doesn't do any lobbying or mass communications. But it has a lot of educational elements."

Of all the lottery websites—each of the state lottery associations, MUSL, etc.—the NASPL website appears to be the most buttoned-up. It has a modern-day design and is packed with information that a curious citizen might appreciate. There are sections about Player Protection (Dawn Nettles would be so proud), responsible gambling, what each jurisdiction does with its lottery revenue, FAQ's, myths, member areas, and more. NASPL also publishes Insights, a free-to-anyone bi-monthly digital PDF magazine filled to the brim with updated metrics on jurisdictional sales performance, articles about members of state commissions, highlights or photos from lottery conferences, and, of course, plenty of advertising from the companies selling lottery terminals, internet games, signage, payment options and more. But it is a professionally designed and informative e-publication.

"It puts on conferences where states come together and get to meet with vendors. The states get to see what the new games are and talk through different ideas about how they can operate as a lottery. Unlike MUSL, NASPL does not produce any games. It's an entity where we come together on issues such as responsible gaming and industry education," Edgar explains.

I finally feel brave enough to ask this burning question: Who actually invents these games?

Walk into any convenience or grocery store and there are usually 10 to 15 different scratch tickets, among other national and state numbers/draw games.

"Each Lottery has teams that are responsible for creating new products and getting them into the marketplace in their jurisdictions.," says Edgar, "but we work closely with our vendors as well. When you get down to running things at the state level, you have two different sides of the product mix. You have your draw games, both multi-state and our own in-state draw games, in Arizona, The Pick, Fantasy Five, and Triple Twist. Most jurisdictions have their own. Some states have Keno, some states have sports betting. And generally, what we have in those types of systems, we work with vendors to provide our equipment and provide our central gaming systems for us. A handful of jurisdictions have created their own systems, but there are three or four primary vendors in the space."

What about scratch tickets?

"That's kind of a separate side of the business. There's three primary companies that do the printing of scratch tickets, IGT, Pollard, and Scientific Games. And again, all of those are contracts that are different in every jurisdiction in terms of who you work with and who you don't. Each jurisdiction makes determinations on which tickets they're going to run. All of us work closely with the vendors because we can get information from them to see how tickets have performed and sold in other jurisdictions. You'll have different levels of competency in each state, too. Some states are more reliant on the vendors, and some of them, like Arizona, have a really strong production team for products. They develop a game completely to make sure it delivers for our jurisdiction."

So it's clear that the states are all very different in their approach. In drawing a contrast between Arizona and Texas, you have Edgar, who is clearly passionate, invested in his role, open, and eager to discuss all things lottery. And then you have the Texas Lottery Commission, who declined to be interviewed at all.

In terms of his day-to-day work, it won't come as a shock to learn that Gregg Edgar wore several hats. But what does an Executive Director of a state lottery commission actually *do*?

"When you look at the executive director role, you're there to make final decisions on everything and really give a vision for where you want the organization to go. Some of the time is spent meeting with retailers, some time is spent working on product development, where we look at and decide what the next thing is that we want to bring to the public. That also means looking at trends and so forth, plus industry research, and interpreting research that's being done for us in terms of what our own players want. In the end, the executive director is responsible."

He adds that one of the larger parts of his role is working on the beneficiary side. This is a side of the lottery that probably isn't understood as much as it should be. Recall at the beginning of this chapter how Edgar lamented the fact that this side of the lottery business isn't communicated clearly or often enough. The beneficiaries of a lottery commission are the individual groups that receive revenue from lottery sales in each state. If a state lottery commission sells $3 million in tickets, they might give away $2 million in prizes to winners. That leaves $1 million in revenue for the state. That $1 million is then allocated for state projects or causes—always allocated for the general good, though it should be argued what that actually means. Many states push their lottery revenue to state education funds. Colorado allocates the revenue to many outdoorsy causes. Delaware pushes funds to different health and social services. It's all public information and a list of each state's revenue allocations are listed on the NAPSL website. And surprise—Edgar has no skin in that game as the Arizona state legislature makes those decisions.

"Arizona is a little bit unique," he explains. "If I'm in California, as an executive there I can go out and I can talk about how all the money goes into education. If you're in Colorado, it's all going into Parks and Recreation and conserving Colorado's unique landscape. Lotteries generally have a maximum of 2 or 3 beneficiaries. Arizona has 17. So I spent a lot of time talking to the media and the public about where the dollars go. For us, with 17 beneficiaries, it's hard to tell that story. So I put quite a bit of time and energy into working with our staff and the public to understand the impact of the Arizona Lottery on our community. The lottery doesn't exist without that beneficiary piece."

He then broke down the numbers for me. "When you work through the flow of Arizona Lottery revenue, about 64 to 65% goes right back to players in wins. Roughly 6.7% goes back to retailers for commissions and the other 19 to 20% goes out to the beneficiaries. Every dollar of profit feeds the beneficiary and that's what is important about what Lottery does—this impact on the community. So when we talk about that from an Arizona perspective, the General Fund in Arizona gets a big chunk, but we also have dollars that go into traffic and transportation needs, to go fix roads and fix streetlights. Over $10,000,000 every year protects Arizona's unique wildlife and landscape through the Arizona Heritage Fund. We also generate $1,000,000 a year towards fighting homelessness."

Edgar saves one of the more meaningful beneficiaries for last, though. Arizona's Court Appointed Special Advocates (CASA) receive their primary budget from the Arizona lottery. These advocates are individuals who volunteer and are trained to work with children who are going into the foster care system. In court, they are the only person who is there solely on behalf of the child. They are the only voice that stands up and specifically states what that child is feeling, thinking, and how they are living at the moment. They are the voice of the child, and a heavy, heavy majority of their whole budget comes from the Arizona lottery. That's not the only child advocacy organization funded by the Arizona lottery, though. There is another program called the Internet Crimes Against Children Task Force. In hearing Edgar talk, it's these programs that draw the most pride and emotion.

"Each state has a similar task force where they're working on getting kids out of sexual exploitation on the Internet. They literally have people sitting at computers all day watching the most horrific things we could ever imagine. And they're trying to locate the child that's being abused. In Arizona, we put $900,000 into that program.

"That $900,000 pays for equipment and pays for the

training of those people who have to sit there. As you can imagine, that's a high-risk position because you have to be able to handle what you're seeing on screens. And then from an equipment standpoint, the bad guys have all of the resources and money, they're able to get the latest and greatest in technology. The money from the lottery tries to level the playing field. This task force is literally saving kids. I mean, $900,000 a year, if we save one kid, it's well worth it. But they save much more than one kid. One year there were over 150 kids who were taken off the Internet by the Arizona task force. Without the lottery, this program is not funded and those kids continue to be victimized."

In exploring the different lottery commission websites, nearly all show their virtuous sides. And while plenty of people are critical of lotteries taking advantage of the poor or downplaying the odds and suckering their hopes and dreams, the beneficiary piece of this is certainly a positive. For many states, this revenue provides a cash spigot that also helps to stave off new taxes on the public as well. U.S. citizens do like that.

Another common question about lottery revenue revolves around unclaimed winnings. This seems more common than one might think. The poorly constructed Powerball website offers up this basic explanation:

"If a Grand Price goes unclaimed, the money must be returned to all lotteries in proportion to their sales for the draw run. The lotteries then distribute the money, based on their own jurisdiction's laws, to other lottery games or to their jurisdiction's general fun, or otherwise as required by law."

There are a variety of reasons certain tickets or winnings may go unclaimed and the most logical one would be a lost ticket. Or perhaps a person had a winning ticket, thought it was a loser, and threw it away. Ouch!

So what happens to all that money that goes unclaimed? It should come as no surprise that Gregg Edgar is an open book about this and expands a bit on the Powerball website blurb.

"Let's start with scratch tickets. We put a scratch ticket out into the marketplace—these have fixed odds. We all know what the build-out of that ticket is going to be and that information is readily available to the player. When that ticket is put out into the marketplace, we set aside the prize money for that product in a separate account, called the prize fund. Every scratch ticket for sale has its prizes set aside at the launch of the game. This is done for the integrity of the operation. When a ticket is claimed, the prize is sitting in that prize fund and it's paid out of the prize fund right away. There's no question about the viability of the ticket."

Walking into a convenience store and seeing a dizzying array of different scratch ticket options may make a person wonder how each of those tickets is actually managed. Why do some scratch tickets stay available for what seems like years and others come and go more quickly? What's the average lifespan of a scratch ticket? Edgar explains this, too.

"It all depends on the price point and odds of the game. It varies quite a bit. So I don't know that I could tell you the exact average lifespan. The $20 Cash Explosion game is one we had in the market fairly regularly. We anticipated and purchased enough tickets for that game to stay in the market for two years. Other ones we build out and they could be in-market for just 12 weeks. We anticipate this by basing it off how tickets have sold in the past. We also know players like new games so we work with retailers to make sure new tickets hit the market on a regular pace. If a game is slowing down in sales, we'll pull back a little bit from marketing it to the retailers to allow other new games to come in. But we'll keep that slower one available so that if there's a retailer that really wants that game, they can order it and make it available."

With scratch tickets, a game is rolled out to the public and there's a mass distribution of tickets sent to retailers. Most state lottery websites will publish stats on an ongoing basis showing how many of the prizes have been won—and how many remain available on that particular ticket. The hardcore lottery gamers who are in-the-know utilize these statistics to influence which scratch ticket they will buy next, helping to increase their odds of winning. Here is an example, taken from the Prizes Remaining page on the Massachusetts Lottery website on October 16, 2023 (obviously these numbers have changed since publishing this book):

Game	Prize Amount	Start	Claimed	Remaining	Game Details
Diamonds and Dollars	$1,000,000 (50K/YR/20YRS)	4	1	3	❭
Universal Monsters ™	$10,000	40	12	28	❭
$10,000,000 Cash Blast	$1,000,000 ($50K/YR/20YRS)	5	1	4	❭
$10,000,000 Cash Blast	$10,000,000 ($500K/YR/20YRS)	3	0	3	❭
Triple Tripler	$10,000	6	2	4	❭
Double Cash	$100,000	6	1	5	❭
777	$1,000,000 ($50K/YR/20YRS)	9	0	9	❭
777	$4,000,000 ($200K/YR/20YRS)	4	0	4	❭
BIG BLUE BONUS CASHWORD	$500,000	4	0	4	❭
$50,000 Star Cashword	$50,000	15	0	15	❭
Bingo	$50,000	10	0	10	❭
Instant $500s	$500	72,016	17,374	54,642	❭
$50 in a Flash	$10,000	12	6	6	❭
$100,000 Extra Play	$100,000	6	1	5	❭

People will steer themselves toward a game with a low number in the claimed column and a high number in the remaining column. So what does a state lottery commission do if the major prizes are paid out right at the beginning of a new game offering? After all, it is a game of odds and it's possible (though unlikely) that all the top jackpot prizes could be won on the first day the ticket is available! That game becomes much less appealing to the public and sales will slow down, fast. That assumes that lots of people are checking on such things. Well, guess who helps to explain that situation? The able and very willing Gregg Edgar.

"We do run a little bit of a risk of the top prizes hitting in the first month of a ticket being out. If that happened, we could be upside down on that product. So we have some controls that disperse winnings across the whole scratch ticket run, but still, it could happen and that would affect the viability of the game over the long haul. But, again, because the prize money is pulled out and separated to begin with, there is no jeopardy for the player. We can't touch that prize money for anything other than paying. But inevitably, people lose tickets. All of Arizona's tickets can be validated for 180 days after the close of a draw or scratch game. So inevitably, you have a certain amount of people who do not claim their prize. People don't bring their tickets in. We've had a couple of larger jackpot prizes in recent years that have been unclaimed. Our statute lays out expressly what we have to do with those monies.

"The majority of it goes right back into the games. We reinvest in the games. Whether it's subsidizing a jackpot level or whether that's increasing the number of wins capable inside of a game. For example, we've recently had some bigger ticket prices with larger prizes. I think it was a six-and-a-half-million-dollar ticket that went unclaimed recently. We turned around and put the money right back into the pick specifically and boosted the jackpots to make it so that the money was going right back to those players."

Money going back into the games is common, but remember, almost everything a state lottery commission does has oversight by state lawmakers. So we took a bit of a long road to get here, but Edgar indicates that unclaimed prize money goes to beneficiaries.

While that does sound generous at the outset, Edgar actually isn't a huge fan of this. "Personally, I would rather they not do that to me. You're messing a little bit with lottery theory and odds there. I'd rather they just stick it all back in the lottery and we'll figure it out from that standpoint."

A swiftly emerging and fast-moving trend in the lottery is, to no one's surprise, the online space. Lottery commissions undoubtedly see many opportunities to expand their gigantic craters full of cash through Internet lotteries, or I-lotteries. With so many people running their lives on a 2x6 inch super-computer in their pocket, it only makes sense that, just like DoorDash and Uber, the lottery will soon follow suit. Some states have already started offering online games to their residents as long as the user registers with a direct connection to their bank and not a credit card. However, state commissions need to be careful—DoorDash and Uber aren't vices in the same way the lottery is. Although having a tasty burrito delivered to my front door without effort approaches vice-like status.

Today, there are ten states that sell lottery tickets online. It's not cut-and-dry, though. Some states enable Powerball players to purchase through sites like Lotto.com, a company that will purchase tickets on behalf of the player and send digital images to confirm. Residents of Oregon are able to use a courier service called The Lotter Oregon. Oklahoma and Indiana allow residents to build tickets on their mobile app, but require players to visit a retailer or lottery vending machine to print the ticket they built. There does not appear to be a universal, consistent way to do this yet.

Gregg Edgar refers to some of these as courier models.

"They're entities that go and sell our tickets, but they do all of the purchasing at retail. I think New York and New Jersey have some laws that allow them to do a straight courier model right away. If you win and the prize is below $600, the courier will just give you your winnings. If the prize is over $600, they'll deliver that ticket to you so you can take it into the jurisdiction to collect."

Kind of seems like DoorDash for lottery.

"So this is coming," Edgar says confidently. "We need to be prepared for it from a public policy standpoint. In some ways, Pandora's box is being opened. Just like sports betting. And you can go do your research on DraftKings and FanDuel, you can see they're losing money like crazy. But the thing I would tell you is they're doing that because they've fundamentally shown that they can change public policy. The conversation that I had with my governor's office was if you're going to open Pandora's box for sports betting, you should have the public policy debate about the broader array of gaming opportunities that exist."

Arizona also has an added wrinkle that not many other states deal with. This state has compacts with the local Native American tribes that determine what gaming can and can't be done. Those compacts are essentially exclusivity agreements with the tribes over gambling regulations and rules.

"I think what you're about to see when you look at FanDuel and DraftKings, the reason these companies are willing to lose billions of dollars on sports betting, is that their next step is to go for e-Gaming or lotteries in some other capacity, and for them to be able to offer you games of chance and any gaming space on your phone. I think that's where they're headed. And maybe the states will wise up and put a higher taxation piece on that. I don't think that's guaranteed, though."

In the end, the governing statute says that the Arizona Lottery has to do things responsibly. FanDuel and DraftKings don't (not that they're not responsible). Edgar has to be focused on the community. And all of the profit, every cent, that the Arizona State Lottery makes goes right back to the designated beneficiaries. At the end of the year, Arizona's lottery business starts back at zero. For-profit companies... not so much.

"Just because of where my profit goes, I have a direct incentive to make our community better programs. I want people to be able to have thriving businesses and do good things, but it is a different model."

Edgar doesn't believe there is anything wrong with profit motives. It is, for all its sheen and blemishes, what drives capitalism after all. The bottom line is that there's a demand for people to have this form of entertainment in their lives. They show it with their wallets. Looking at the lottery commissions, though, there are actually controls that are in place. A state-sanctioned online lottery system can put limits on how often or how much money people bet. FanDuel and DraftKings surely aren't doing that, they're letting the individual players set daily limits.

While discussing the ins and outs of gaming and ethics, the subject of consumer advocacy comes up. Gregg Edgar has heard of Dawn Nettles, but isn't terribly familiar with the saber-rattling she gets into with the Texas Lottery Commission. Assuming that not every state has a Dawn Nettles, there must be entities or individuals nationwide who sound alarms about the morals and intentions of state lottery commissions.

"Arizona was the first lottery west of the Mississippi and was enacted by public referendum. The people voted on it in 1980 and it was a very close vote. As part of an agency sunsetting, Lottery went in front of the public again and it was renewed with a much higher percentage margin than the original vote. So I think in Arizona we've got a mindset that people want to play the lottery and so long as the agency is operated responsibly and with integrity, it will remain a source of revenue for the state. Now, when we talk about expansion with an I-lottery or Keno there are definitely folks who are against it, but that goes back to what I was talking about in the beginning of our conversation—you need to have the public policy discussion. You need to have that open debate of what we, as a community, want or don't want. And everybody's got a voice at that table. The Center for Arizona Policy is an entity that has been very anti-gaming, not just lottery. They're anti any kind of gaming or vice issues in the state. It's a voice that needs to be at the table. To me, if we have the broader discussion about impacts on the community, in the end, the positive that the lottery brings is hard to argue against. By the same token, you have to hold the agency accountable for the integrity and responsible approach to its operations. People enjoy playing the games. They might not be people who like to go to the movies. They might not like to go out for dinner, but they would like to sit down and dream about the opportunity of winning something big."

Edgar finishes off our conversation with a bang.

"What I would like to take apart is why aren't we, as a society, doing better about teaching people about finance and managing money. And I think we can look at that from a much broader perspective even than the massive win perspective. You know, we could all be doing better in how we teach our children to manage their money. When I dealt with winners, I always asked, before they finalized their documents, 'did you talk to an accounting professional? Did you talk to a lawyer? Did you consult a financial advisor to give you some perspective on the best ways to set yourself up for success?' I said that every time I talked to them. We were doing some outreach to large banking institutions that are very well-respected to ask if there are some things that we can do together to drive some financial literacy. Connecticut has done some work on this locally, but the national effort had not moved forward before my departure. It's an objective that I think we need to get to personally."

Hear, hear!

It shouldn't shock anyone that Edgar wasn't allowed to play any lottery games that were sold in Arizona during his tenure. He could go to another state and buy a California State Lottery game such as scratch tickets or daily numbers, but he wasn't not allowed to play Powerball or Mega Millions anywhere, given those are national games. Something to think about if you see a plum job opportunity at your local state lottery commission—your odds go from barely existent to nil.

CHAPTER SEVEN

The Lottery Lawyer

You have probably never heard of Kurt Panouses. He's not admired by millions of people (sorry, Kurt). But this is a guy you should want to know. Why? Because if you work with him, you've won the lottery.

You have also probably never heard of Indialanctic, Florida. This is a tiny town of 3,010 people, not as reported by the National Weather Service, but per the official 2020 United States Census report[42]. Word has it that the National Weather Service is far busier in Florida covering its myriad of disruptive events, weather and otherwise.

This small town is part of Brevard County, located on central Florida's east coast and attached to the Palm Bay-Melbourne-Titusville metropolitan statistical area. It is here that you will find Kurt, the self-appointed Lottery Lawyer. As of writing this book, Kurt has represented over 30 lottery winners, including handling one of the largest Powerball jackpots ever ($1.58 Billion), and other massive winnings worth $1.05 billion (Mega Millions) and $516 million. With 35 years of experience in state lottery laws, statutes, and multi-

---

[42] https://data.census.gov/all?q=indialantic,+fl

state lottery agreements, Panouses is a true authority and an expert in handling large windfalls of cash. He has certifications in wills, trusts, estate laws and of course, is a Certified Public Accountant. He is also a regular contributor to lottery stories on Good Morning America, CBS News, ABC News, and plenty other major news media outlets. If you win Powerball or MegaMillions, you are a) incredibly lucky, b) shell-shocked, and c) in immediate need of Kurt before you do anything else. He is your guy. Rent a private jet and go meet him, you can afford it now.

"Anyone can take you through the claims process," he explains, "It's a bunch of documents. The problem is that the people who win have never dealt with financial people before —attorneys, lawyers and planners—and they don't know how to react. If there's no one there to quarterback the whole thing, it's a problem. When you get to a stumbling block, you need options. You need to have a game plan, follow a game plan, and be ready to change. A lot of people can help with parts of the process, but you really need a Q.B."

It's probably not too hard to guess that being the Lottery Lawyer wasn't Panouses's childhood dream; at 6'4", that dream was more about basketball. His intention for college was to play hoops, but he quickly saw the divide between high school and college basketball and knew the college game wasn't for him.

"I realized that playing college basketball was not fun like it was in high school. It was a job. And it took away from any opportunity to have any fun or do anything other than that during that six-month time period," he says.

So it was on to his next goal, to get an accounting degree. He did just that and began working in accounting for a couple of years to build up some experience. Then back into school for law, specializing in taxes.

"I came out with a CPA and a law degree then started

working for a big CPA firm, Pricewaterhouse, in Chicago. I did that for a couple of years and then ended up coming down to Florida, where I was going to be an estate planning attorney. So here I am, 30-something years old, a state planning attorney, doing wills, trusts, and estates. It's kind of like a practice where people die and other people inherit wealth. So it's really not much different from someone buying a lottery ticket out of the blue."

He readily admits that the Lottery Lawyer moniker was dumb luck. A small amount of lottery business started coming his way and things snowballed from there. Eventually, he began taking winners up to Tallahassee to help them with the claims process, money collection, and all of the other steps involved in claiming lottery winnings in person. These were not wins in the hundreds of millions yet, but Panouses gathered expertise in lottery claims.

Panouses adds, "After a while, you realize that you may have this purpose that some higher power puts in front of you. And either you take the life raft or you don't."

Even with a few lottery winner experiences under his belt, it wasn't as if he had hung a 20'x20' banner outside the law office window with dollar signs and lottery cards on it. He wasn't pushing hard to actively recruit or land more lottery business. It wasn't until 2016 when a winner in Melbourne Beach, FL won the big one. Powerball. And still, that winner first called a different attorney. That other attorney, however, knew someone who had some experience in lottery winnings and recommended the guy over in Indialanctic. Panouses got the call and ended up handling a monster lottery win.

"It was a learning process," Panouses says. "After that one, I got to understand it more and thought about how quarterbacks function in these big games. Because when you go into a game for the first time, you're really edgy. You don't know what to expect. And then after you're there, it's a metamorphosis and then after a while, it doesn't bother you anymore. It's 'I can handle anything.' You know, it doesn't matter what gets thrown at me. But after 2016, I started getting a lot more calls."

Panouses smelled an opportunity and started to think about the marketing side of his practice. He worked with an agency on retainer for a while and the Lottery Lawyer was born. The agency (and Panouses) kicked off a marketing blitz to create awareness and utilized popular Google search keywords like "Powerball lawyer" and "Mega Millions lawyer" to drive interest. Things started moving.

"It was the point in my career where I'm in my sixties and I started asking myself: do I do five wills for people during a week, or do I handle one lottery win for someone? And what's more fun—these people who are going to pass away or lottery winners? These people are getting money in the best way. So it's a fun practice and I just got to the point where I figured I would rather do lottery work and have maybe ten clients a year as opposed to having 100 estate plans. I think that decision to actively market it and get some assistance in that area was paying off."

Today, Panouses still helps existing clients, the ones he's had over his 30 years in the business, but it's largely low maintenance. His focus is lottery clients.

"I'll get calls and handle about 10 to 12 jackpots per year that are over $5 million dollars, and they're all in different states. So that's what it has turned into. I have probably three or four families that won a lot of money. I mean, ungodly amounts of money. And I'm likely the only person who knows who they are," he adds.

Putting winning aside for a second, Panouses likes to call the lottery a tax on people who mostly can't afford to pay it. In most states, the profits generated from the lottery are used in part to pay for school systems. This is revenue where if there wasn't a lottery, the general population would instead be paying those taxes. But since the lottery does generate a lot of its revenue from lower-income people with a dream, Panouses contends that it *is* a poor man's tax for the most part.

"Right now one of the lotteries is getting big. Powerball is like $700 million this weekend," he says, "so I'll start getting calls from people that are saying, 'hey, will I win? I'm bringing you in to help me with the process. I just wanted to talk to you in advance.' So they think that they're going to win! Divine intervention or something. Or they have these crazy stories that they'll call me up with. You want to be nice to all of these people because you certainly don't want to shut down their dreams. But it's very difficult to answer those things and be helpful because you just honestly think that these people just don't have any idea of the odds that they're playing against."

Panouses, probably more than any other lawyer in the U.S., has met more overnight multi-millionaires (and billionaires!) at virtually the very moment they've won. They're stunned, they don't know what to do next, they're nervous, and probably scared. Whip that all up with overwhelming elation, and you've got an emotional slurry. All of these feelings swirling around at the very moment Kurt gets to first meet them. Fun, yes, but also a heavy burden that is not to be taken lightly. Panouses enters someone's life at perhaps the batshit craziest point of existence.

He explains the mindset of a winner, based on his experiences: "There is a large spread of feelings. What I have found is that the people who have won these really large jackpots, like over $100 million, for me they've always been older people. So they're not 20-year-olds. They're 50 and 60-year-olds who are winning these for the most part. Once you tell them that we're going to put together a good plan and that we need three or four weeks, they start to relax…a little bit. I get them to understand that and explain that they may have to live with that feeling of anxiety for another 3 to 4 weeks. I'll tell them they're not going to sleep. For that matter, I'm not going to sleep either, because I'm going to be constantly thinking about things that we should do and could do, or how we're going to go about it."

He explains to these winners that the money is not coming tomorrow because a lot needs to happen in order to correctly set up a winner. Panouses says it takes a few days for that to sink in and eventually they start to get a little more comfortable. The process moves along and the winners are kept informed at every step by Panouses, who explains what he is doing and why he is doing it.

"They don't get worried again until the day of the claim or the day before the claim when all of this stuff suddenly has to happen," he explains.

"1 may know the people in different state lottery commissions I've worked with before. So I'll tell the winner that we're going to walk into this building and this is what it's going to look like. This is what we're going to do first. We're going to go here. We're going to go there. And here is where you're going to meet this person. I'll schedule out the whole day in advance. And once we get through that process, they get more relaxed because now they're seeing it—their quarterback's been here before."

Panouses goes into some detail on the process, explaining that it's just getting to know the client and getting some color into their lives. This will be very important as he draws up the playbook. Do they have kids? How old are they? Are their kids married? Do they have problems in their marriages? These questions are important because unless the winner is very foolish, they're not going to spend all the money they've won. It's going to pass through a generation. And likely multiple generations. Panouses likes to spread it out into what he calls a club format. Keeping in mind that his clients are usually in their 50s and 60s and are parents, he'll set it up so that 60 to 70% of the winnings is in the parent's name and the kids have the other 30 to 40%. This way it is not considered a gift, which saves the family a boatload of money in potential taxes, as gifts are taxed. So the winner actually becomes a family unit, or club, that claims the ticket. The taxes are spread out and everyone has their own little pile of money.

This assumes the family is cohesive and stable, of course. That's not always the case. Stepping into any family dynamic is complicated enough, but imagine doing it while clutching a winning lottery ticket for, say, $500 million dollars. Fraught with potential complications seems like an understatement. Taking all of this into account, Panouses has to factor in other pieces: where the kids live, what's their lifestyle, do they have issues that may necessitate restricting how the winnings are set up for them. Sometimes winners don't want to set aside money for their kids at all. That must be a doozy. There are even occasions where Panouses requires non-disclosure agreements to be signed before he will even talk to them. The Lottery Lawyer is a stickler for his clients and their anonymity.

But how important is the anonymity piece for his clients?

"I won't accept a client who wins a billion dollars and wants to go on TV the next day and claim it. I'll have nothing to do with that. I've learned that people who do that are loose cannons and all that's going to do is fall back on me as the attorney or the advisor for not advising them appropriately."

Panouses has seen firsthand the overwhelming amount of attention given to lottery winners who go public. Recall

James Hayes having to go to the post office daily for the six pounds of mail he received. Or the father with AIDS who showed up at his house with his two young daughters, begging Hayes to take them and give them a good life. Public lottery winners are subject to non-stop begging, emails, letters, phone calls, and visits from desperate people and charities.

There's also a common scam where imposters claim to be the winner. These imposters set up social media profiles in the lottery winner's name, with the winner's actual photos, and then they post on Facebook or Twitter that they're "giving away some of their fortune to 50 lucky people." All those 50 lucky people have to do is contact the lottery winner and share their bank account information. It's hard to believe people fall for it, but they do. In spades.

This is part of the reason why the logo for the Lottery Lawyer looks like a shield. He feels it is his job to protect these winners from the endless stream of communication and abuse from the nefarious and the desperate. And that means doing everything and anything to keep the winner completely anonymous. This even includes holding big checks at lottery commission news conferences. A cursory Google search bears this out:

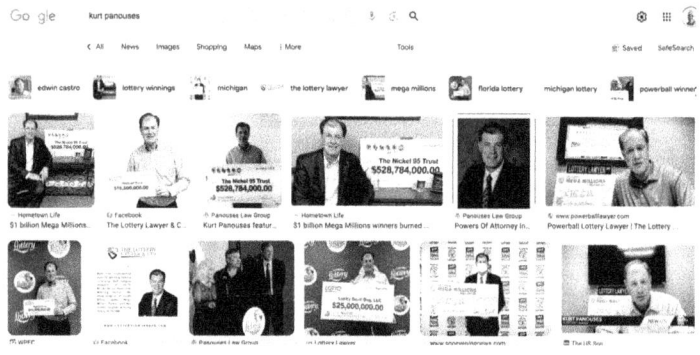

With all of those pictures on Google and his name being attached to lottery winners, Panouses is also the occasional target for scammers, who will pose as him.

He adds, incredulously, "Even in my little hometown when I get ready to make a major claim for someone, I call all my kids and family members and tell them what's going to happen and when. I ask them to please be on the lookout because I don't want one of my family members to be thought of as a major winner where they could be attacked. So I just tell the kids to be on high alert for when our name gets out there, even though it's not me that's winning because it looks to someone like I'm the winner."

For all of these reasons, and more, Panouses does his best to keep the winner's identity anonymous.

"It's very important that you have this dialogue with them, get them to open up to you and feel comfortable opening up to you about this process. It's very frustrating when I read stories about people who just go public and claim it. That's going to be a real problem for those people who go on TV. They don't know what their life is going to be like. I get calls and letters all the time from people and they're very very difficult stories, especially families that need money. They need a loan, they need this and they need that. I shield my clients from all of that."

So yes, looking at it from a high level, working with lottery winners can be fun. But this part, being a shit umbrella for clients, is probably the least satisfying part of the job. But it is part of the package Panouses offers. And it's all done to keep his clients lives as normal as possible.

But not all states allow winners to be anonymous. There are roughly ten states that allow it straight out and there are another twenty or so states he's dealt with where there are extra steps to get there, but anonymity is attainable. Even for states that don't say a winner can claim their winnings anonymously, Panouses has been able to find some options.

"If you know what you're doing, you can figure out a way through their rules to be in compliance, but also keep it anonymous," he says. "The problem is, and what most people don't understand and what a lot of attorneys without experience don't understand, is that's only part of it. What I've learned is that a lawyer might think they've done it anonymously, but people can put in a public records request and still get all the information about winners, even if they did it through an LLC or a trust. And I bet you that their lawyer didn't do enough where this information could be kept from a public records request. And so that's why, when I set these things up, I do multiple layers so that even if you get through one layer, you're not getting to the second or third layer. And sometimes the clients ask why I'm making it so complicated. And the lottery office wants to know why I'm making it so complicated. Well, if someone made a public records request, they could get this information and you'd have to give it to them. That's the one thing that I fear for a lot of these winners. That's why you need a quarterback who has been there."

Assuming that you've done the right thing and chartered a plane to meet him immediately, here is the list of things Kurt Panouses will run through before you claim your winnings.

- Do not sign or mark the ticket. This gives him a clean slate on which to paint the client's picture
- Take your time to decide on annuity or lump sum (you have 60 days to choose)
- Discuss family and friends (who should know or not know about this)

- How should we claim the winnings (trust, LLC, group, etc.)

- Have fun with claim day (like going to Disney World!)

- Decide whether you will tip the lottery commission off that you're coming, or just show up and surprise them

- Don't leave a trail. Always rent a vehicle and have a driver

- Get in and out quickly (no opportunity for someone to take a photo)

- Always mask up, wear a hat, sunglasses, even a Halloween mask/costume

So, you have met with Pansouses. The whirlwind is dying down. The claim day has come and gone. The claim was accepted in a perfect Gumby costume, and the money is deposited. All done, right? Hardly. There is lots of important work still to come.

This is where Panouses's 30-plus years of experience as a CPA, tax expert, and estate planner kick into gear. After all, a massive lottery winner now sits on an overwhelming fortune and there are a lot of complicated things that will come into play quickly. His next task is to put a vehicle together to help winners do what they're trying to do.

"I try to ask them, where do you see yourself six months from now? Do you see your life staying in the same neighborhood? Do you see yourself going to a bigger house in a different part of the state or country? Where do you expect to be? Where do your kids expect to be? Because I try to put all that into a results-oriented plan for them," he says. "We were able to accomplish what we needed to accomplish, and that was to get them to claim the ticket anonymously and have some peace of mind. And then after that, they realize I'm still the most important professional in their life."

It's at this point where Panouses does his work to hammer

the nail home and get his clients to take full advantage of the old adage "set for life."

"Well, you know, people who win $300 million, $500 million, they don't need a 20% return, you know? They really want the comfort of knowing that this money's there. I just got done meeting with one of these big clients last week and their financial people were there talking about the returns that they're getting on investments, blah, blah, blah," he says. "And I told them, we're really not interested in getting those returns. We want safe. We're talking about people who are 60 or 70 years old! They're never going to go through that much money. It's not their plan to make more money or give more taxes to our government. They just want to know that everything's comfortable."

For Panouses, the shorter goal is to just live with the money for six months to a year, enjoy it when needed, and see what situation the winner is in after year one. He says person's approach to money management and finance typically stays pretty consistent, regardless of if they won the money or if they inherited it.

"If they were spenders before, they're going to be spenders now; that's not going to change. If they were money hoarders before, they're going to be hoarders now. I always tell people that my rule of thumb is to spend 3%. You know, if you can live on a budget of 3% or 4% of your money, you'll never even touch the principle. You should spend that! That means you have a little extra money to fly private jets. Let's get you used to that. Let's join a country club. Let's do the fun things in life. Because if you don't spend it, your kids will," he says with a laugh.

Panouses adds that regardless of whether it's an inheritance from a relative or winning the lottery, most people still have mortgages, credit card debt, and other financial obligations before they come into money and they find themselves going through new money very quickly. He agrees that there is often a mentality that their winnings or inheritances are free money and therefore they tend to spend it more irresponsibly. A bit of human nature. This is part of why Panouses strongly encourages any newly-minted millionaire to really understand a budgeting system and check in at six months or a year.

"Right," he says. "Let's have no huge purchases. Write a list of things you bought, and then at the end of the six months or year, let's take a look at it, have a meeting, and say 'did you really need that?' We try to just get them into a situation where they get to a comfort level and get what they really want. If I can get them to the first year, then we can take a look at what their income was vs. what they spent during the year."

That becomes the next major point in a winner's journey with Panouses; getting them comfortable with a loose spending limit based on income. If a person gets to a point where they understand the benefits of that 3 to 4% guidance after that first year, that's a big win. Panouses shared a story of one client who couldn't include certain family members in a claim because of their marriage situation. The winner just figured they'd pass a gift to them but didn't totally comprehend the gift tax implications of such a thing.

"I had to explain it to them this way," he says. "You buy pizza with ten slices of pizza in the box and you decide you want to give two slices to your brother. So you take the two slices out and you give it to your brother. How much do you have left in the box? Eight? No. Because when you gave the two to your brother, we had to lose a piece and a half to taxes, we had to just throw that piece-and-a-half in the garbage. So sometimes it's hard for people to understand all these things that they have now found themselves in because they've never been coached before by a professional. They didn't have private bankers or tax accountants before. They never had lawyers, never had planners, never had wealth. And now they're put in this position and some of them just think they can do whatever they want. And it's my job to rein them in so that they they can live their life comfortably and have the peace of mind without throwing away huge amounts of pizza."

Panouses then swings back to the importance of anonymity. It's clear he believes this is far and away the most important piece of the puzzle when it comes to working with large sums of cash. Once someone is exposed to the public in any way, it's very much like ants sniffing out the picnic. Suddenly people are everywhere. Friends, family members, neighbors, and charities, and they are all knocking. Most of the time Panouses takes the brunt of the inquiries, bless him. He's used to it now, it seems. Random requests for $100,000 here and there or asking for money to invest in one product or another. It seems like he's heard it all…and then some.

"If it's something that I think is legitimate, where it's educational or something like that or something like a need for a community, I'll just give a quick call to the winner and ask what they think about it or if it's something we should throw in our charitable fund," he explains.

It doesn't sound like much ever gets through to the winners, though. Case in point: Panouses refuses to pass along any messages to his clients from me about being interviewed anonymously in this book.

Then there's the conversation people have so often with others about what they would do if they won the lottery. Many times it's "I'd give X% away to charity!" or "I'd give half of it away." Panouses also sets the record straight on how much of that is just talk and how much is real.

"The mind frame of people is that they're going to have a

$100 million and they're going to give 20% away. Or I watch TV and they're interviewing people on the street and talking to them about the billion-dollar ticket this weekend and they say they're to give a third to charity, a third to their family, and keep a third. You know, everyone talks about charitable giving. But once they get this money in, all of a sudden now it's kind of changed a little bit. If they have certain charities that they've helped before, we'll try to figure out how we get some money to those charities."

Even then, Panouses will strongly recommend any donations be done anonymously, as the scammers do watch charitable giving for specific names of people to potentially prey on. For charitable giving, he strongly encourages winners to set up gift-giving funds, almost like separate accounts that the winners put funds into. From there, a winner can just tell Panouses to give an amount anonymously to a specific organization, drawn from the fund. But when it comes to setting up entire foundations or philanthropic entities for giving, Panouses says it's mostly all talk.

"Some people say they want to set up a foundation. Well, when I talk to them about that and tell them what's involved with a foundation and all the work and I ask which family members are going to keep it going, that's where it starts becoming a little murky for them," he laughs a little, "and their idea of setting up a foundation quickly becomes 'I don't want to do that work.'

"It seems like most people give a couple of thousand dollars a year to various organizations. I do have one client and every year she gives away $500,000 or $600,000. Big ticket items. But now that we told her about just setting up one of these community funds and it's just an anonymous gift from there, it's much easier for her to do that."

He adds one more note on charitable giving. "So they all

talk about charity, but after six months, they kind of like seeing that big number in their bank account," he smiles. "And yes, they do give some to charity. But it's not at the level that everyone thinks it is. It's certainly not at the level that everyone *says* they're going to do early on. It's a small percentage and it's not the 20 or 30% that everyone talks about before they win."

As the conversation continued, we got to the topic of the various state lottery commissions across the U.S.A. Panouses has his own viewpoints on the state commissions and they are, perhaps surprisingly, more in line with those of Dawn Nettles. In fact, Panouses believes strongly that we need *more* people like Dawn Nettles in the United States, people who keep an eye on lotteries in an effort in to help the public.

The Lottery Lawyer feels that the states are perhaps leaning a little too hard into the volume of games offered. The notion is that people keep buying them, so why not keep selling them? It is, after all, a genius way to raise money without pissing off the residents by raising taxes. In short, he thinks there are just too many games. He may have a point. Just picture again the lottery options on display when walking into a convenience store. It's quite an array. But is it good for us to have so many? Well, beauty is in the eye of the beholder: some are disgusted by it, whereas other players get a sparkle in their eyes. Or maybe it's dollar signs in their eyes like they used to show in old cartoons.

If there are 20 different scratch tickets to choose from, that must mean there's more winning in that big pile. Psychologically, that person seeing dollar signs isn't likely thinking about the similar lottery displays in the three other convenience stores and gas stations in town. And the thousands of lottery displays scattered amongst the state. There probably isn't more winning in that single store. Just more options to lose.

And the state commissions? They have a job to do: drive profit to fund those state pet programs, and do it with as high a margin as possible. What does that mean to Panouses? Run things lean.

"When you look at state lottery commissions, there are a couple of high-end people. The commissioner, legal, the claims division manager, there's like four or five people that are making a good salary. Everyone else is a little bit above minimum wage. They're not making much."

It all has the makings for state lottery commissions that may not run optimally. Remember how James Hayes walked into the California Lottery offices and saw that the clerk was the same guy who also worked at a local KMart?

Panouses says that when he walks into a state commission office, he is rarely, if ever, dealing with an attorney or director. He's dealing with a low-paid lottery clerk, likely making a little bit over minimum wage. His sense is that they are older, long-time state workers who get solid benefits based on the number of years served. They may have worked in other, more difficult state offices and decided to close out their careers in the lottery office, because it's just easier on the psyche than, say, seeing all the heartbreak while working in the family & children division. It's a theory, and a logical one. He's also seen a lot of inexperienced people working at state lottery commissions and, of course, those people aren't allowed to play, so they may not even be terribly familiar with the games and operations.

All of this adds up to what Panouses calls "a false sense of legitimacy" directed at the state commissions and he cites his own state commission as evidence. "I'll go up to Tallahassee sometimes and I'll bring a claim in and they'll just pull out one of my old files because they figure they should just do it the same way, and they'll look to just copy things over. They don't provide any guidance. The only people who are really making the money are the elite at the very top."

He goes on to lament the whole marketing end of it, all the winning tickets on the walls at the commissions, and a lack of real experience or expertise at the commissions, and how it all adds up to many people just thinking the whole thing is rigged, much the same way Dawn Nettles feels about the lottery brass in Texas.

Panouses references the massive Powerball drawing in January 2023. The drawing that evening was delayed and the winning numbers weren't drawn until the next day. That raised a lot of suspicions amongst the public that something was amiss or there was a scam in place.

"And now's it been over 60 days and no one's claimed that winning ticket yet. These lotteries are doing themselves in by the way they're operating. I also think with the number of games, down the road, there is going to be a judge that's going to say this was all done improperly."

As if channeling Dawn Nettles, Panouses continues, "I've seen tickets where you scratch everything off and you look and you read every single number and there's no winner. But then to be certain, the person takes it over to the machine and they put it in the machine and the machine says it is a winner. I've seen times when the machine says the ticket is a $50 dollar or even a $1,000 winner. But the bar code says it's a $20 winner. And this company that makes these games, they're mass producing them for all these different states, which means multiple states are going to have these same issues. Sooner or later, someone is going to sue a state lottery and be successful. People already call me up and they want me to help sue a lottery. I don't have time to do that. I'm not a civil litigation attorney."

But there are plenty of enterprising attorneys who would take the case if they see a chance for cash. Just think about all the personal injury lawyers buying up TV commercial time in local markets. Panouses thinks that's what's going to happen. He believes that an attorney will eventually take it on and file a claim. With all the mutual agreements and multi-state agreements tied to lotteries across the country now, Panouses believes lottery issues are ripe for some good old ambulance chasing.

"These state commissions just don't help themselves. And I think what we're going to find is there's going to need to be some reduction in these games at the state levels because everyone is suspecting that it's a scam. And, you know, the secrecy of it all is not helping, either. It used to be you would have your state lottery, and the drawing would air on TV with a CPA there managing it. Now it's all being held in private rooms."

"I'm concerned about the future of the lottery because I think they're doing themselves in, to be honest with you. And I think the way they're going about it with the number of games and the cost of some of them…I mean, there's now $50 scratch-off tickets!"

Offer it up, though, and they'll buy it. Sell that American dream. History keeps hitting that hammer over and over again and people just keep buying these tickets and they think they're going to win. Spend $50 for ten scratch tickets, maybe one of them is a $10 winner. Take that $10 and buy two more tickets. Because they might win again. But the fact is that they're already down $40 bucks from the first purchase. And the red just keeps getting redder. They don't look at it as a loss. And that's a problem. Any small win is never free money. Ever.

Another thing that bothers Panouses are lottery pools. These are very common occurrences where a group of people, usually at a place of employment, pool their money together, buy a large pile of lottery tickets, and then split the winnings. The obvious theory is that buying 100 tickets instead of two tickets improves the chances of winning. While that might be mathematically true, when you think about a single number having a 1 in 292 million chance of hitting, the odds on 100 tickets aren't much of an improvement. Entering into a work pool also lends itself to potential sabotage and nasty trust issues among a group.

"I don't like it," Panouses says. His lawyerly brain takes over. "You need to have a written agreement. Pools always have a deep end. Don't do an office pool unless you document it with a written agreement."

Throughout our lengthy conversation, Panouses seems to have an aw-shucks mentality about it all. He didn't set out to become a well-known Lottery Lawyer and he seems to have a sense of borderline incredulousness about some of the processes he goes through and the blind trust that people put in him.

"Here's what really blows my mind. I'm down here in Florida and I'll get a call from a winner of $5 million dollars in Ohio. They've never met me before. We'll talk on the phone on a Monday and I'm ready to go by Friday. So I'll fly up to Ohio. They'll meet me at the hotel where I might be staying. We'll talk for a little bit and then they will actually hand me their ticket, unsigned. I mean, just think that through! They read about me somewhere, they don't know me and they just give me a ticket worth $5 million dollars! I'll take it, put it in my briefcase, and I'll leave them at the hotel and walk to the state lottery office a couple of blocks away. I'll go inside and sign in. Then I'll go up to the lottery office, sign all the paperwork to claim it for them in the entity of the trust or whatever we're doing, and then come back and a check is delivered to them like a week later."

People have so much confidence in Panouses that they do all of this without knowing who he is because they might have a friend who says they have heard of Kurt. Or they did a Google search. But he remains astounded and amazed that people can just implicitly trust a stranger with millions of their dollars. Panouses is very grateful for it and also describes the multi-directional appreciation he and his clients have for each other after they win.

"It's so important to me to have that trust when it comes to talking to people. I'm a legal person. I helped them with the process, we kept them anonymous and they will have questions in the future. So I get involved with assisting them with their questions or helping them through a dilemma. They want to buy property. They want to do some charitable thing. So I interface with them on things like that and that's probably half of my time. And then maybe 10% of my time is existing estate plans and then the other 40% is really-new lottery clients."

It's that initial trust and confidence in him that keeps the relationship going. A winner gets very comfortable financially, but perhaps more cautious generally. Panouses has worked with them through every step and this gives them a level of comfort and trust that they will value, likely forever. Panouses is not just a lawyer, but a guide to being suddenly wealthy.

"They never had wealth before," he says. "They sometimes don't know what the appropriate tip amount is for a caddie after golf or for a waiter after a great steak dinner. They're learning the process and I'm helping them. They've never bought a $300 bottle of wine. A lot of them really have to figure it out and they have to learn what it's like to be wealthy and it can be difficult."

A problem, by the way, that pretty much anyone in the world would be happy to take on.

Panouses says most of his clients slowly figure it out, though. He refers back to his advice to winners early on; try to spend 3% a year and see where they are at the end of the first year.

After that first year, that's when he'll start telling them it's okay to fly first class or even private if they want. Because of COVID, he says that more of his clients want a private plane that will show up at their local airport. They don't want to deal with multiple connections, wearing masks, and a mass of people. Their health is important. So he will also help them get medical providers who offer concierge medicine where they pay around $5,000 a year and they have a doctor who is available 24 hours a day and will deliver medicine to their doorstep.

"So if you did come down with COVID and you tested positive, you call this doctor and you tell them what your temperature is," he explains, "and on a Zoom call, the doctor will just let them know to open their box and take two white pills for COVID."

Panouses adds that once they start seeing that and they see that there are companies out there that help them with pretty much anything, they feel a lot more comfortable in their life. But it takes time. They need a game plan from their quarterback. They need to know what's appropriate to pay at this level of wealth to a bank or a financial group. Is it 20 basis points on earnings? 30 basis points? Panouses leans towards the conservative. After all, they've already gotten the ultimate return on their lottery ticket investment. But he'll get permission to have the bank send him copies of all of his client's statements so that he can review them every month to stay current on his client's lives.

"So I continue to help out on a monthly basis. Someone needs to do that for them because they're not used to doing it," he says.

* * *

Not all of his clients are gigantic jackpot winners, either. The clients who've won hundreds of millions are certainly more time-consuming by necessity, but he also has a strong group of clients who've won $1 million or $5 million on scratch tickets. After taxes, these wins aren't enough to facilitate an utter sea-change in people's lives, so Panouses says they're more in a hurry to get the process over with so they can get back to their life again. A smaller win can be wrapped up within a week. This is typically because there is less of a need to include other people in decisions.

"I just want to have the respect of my clients and my peers. If I can do this, they feel comfortable sending new work my way," Panouses says, "I get calls from people that I handled a $1,000,000 ticket for three years ago, and they're calling me because they have some issue. I just feel blessed that they still have confidence in me even though I haven't done anything for them in three years."

And how does a Lottery Lawyer get paid, anyway? One might think that it's party time for the lawyers, given the truckload of dollars that are pulling into the dock. While there's no denying that the lottery is a lucrative game and being a lawyer can provide a well-compensated living, it's probably not what you think. Panouses explains that it's not anything like a personal injury lawyer who gets nothing or gets $50 million.

"No, no, that doesn't happen," he says with a laugh. "I look at it like an agent for a football player or a baseball player. You know, I don't throw a pitch, but the agent might make 1 to 4%. I'll take a look at how much money they won, what our game plan is going to be and if it's a family or a larger group, I'll come up with a flat fee arrangement. At these big big levels, it's clearly under 1%. But when I tell this to a client, they'll say they were ready to pay 20%. No, you're not going to pay someone 20%! But that's just for the claims process."

He goes on to explain that after he gets them through the first tax return, things open up and if they want him to stay on board, they work together to come up with a monthly fee and Panouses takes care of them on an ongoing basis. Not all clients take this option, but "most do," Panouses says.

"They like to know that someone's looking at stuff for them—what the investment people are charging or what the CPA is doing."

The quarterback leads the team.

With all that winning surrounding Panouses, you might wonder if he plays the lottery himself.

"I do," he says, "I mean, I'll put some $10 or $20 scratch tickets in Christmas cards and birthday cards for my staff at the office. Same at the holidays for my family. It's almost like a joke for me at this point because I'll also put my business card in there, too, and tell them to make sure they call me if they win." He laughs at that but then adds, "It should never be your plan to win, though. It shouldn't be your retirement plan."

CHAPTER EIGHT

Organized Crime

Here's a shocker. Organized crime has managed to infect and de-legitimize lotteries on many occasions. Entire books could be written on the subject.

According to 2005's 454-page Encyclopedia of White Collar & Corporate Crime[43], organized crime in the lottery goes as far back as America's colonial days. That's right. Crooked lotteries were a thing even before electricity. Just picture Tony Soprano in a powdered wig.

One of the earliest documented occasions of crime infiltrating the lottery goes all the way back to 1823 and involves the U.S. Congress, according to the aforementioned Encyclopedia. There are so many potential and easy jokes to make knowing that it involved Congress, but refraining seems like the best and most professional approach for now. Alas, Congress were not the perpetrators anyway. In this case, they merely created this specific lottery, which was set up to raise funds for a beautification project in Washington D.C. You don't have to be a genius to figure out what happened next. The organizers took off with the proceeds and the

---

[43] General Editor: Laurence M. Salinger, Ph.D

lottery was never paid out. Apparently, taking off with the proceeds is a long-standing tradition in D.C..

Another story from the Encyclopedia details some shenanigans in Louisiana, where it was discovered that the entity operating the Louisiana state lottery was actually a New York-based group of criminal minds. The New York syndicate was skimming off the top of ticket purchases and paying off Louisiana state officials to continue letting the New Yorkers operate the lottery in the Bayou.

The aforementioned incidents in the 1800s were just two of many that caused numerous U.S. states to start outlawing lotteries outright. As with the 13 years of alcohol prohibition in the United States, once the official state lotteries were shut down, illegal lotteries popped up. As predictable as day and night. Plenty of those illegal numbers games run by organized crime groups continue unabated through, well, today. In addition to the illegal numbers games, organized crime groups have also managed to stay involved in the now-legal state lotteries. They do this through involvement in terminal supplies like lottery machines and other lottery-related services in various states.

But let's go back to the illegal numbers games from the 1800s. According to the Encyclopedia, some lotteries in the 1800s cost in excess of $60 per ticket, whereas the average annual income in America at the time was sub-$1000 per year. These re-launched state lotteries were a game of the upper class. Naturally, there was a void to fill for industrious criminals, as the lower-income earners couldn't stomach (or risk sharing the news with their spouse) that they were spending 6% of their annual income in one day on a single ticket.

Illegal policy betting took off and the low-earners were welcomed into the hopes and dreams of winning cash by criminals. These daily numbers games were not connected whatsoever with state-sanctioned lotteries and the game was simple—the player picks three digits to match a set of three winning numbers picked at random the following day. In order to give players confidence that the numbers were legitimate, the winning numbers would just match something particular from the day of the drawing, such as the last three numbers of the value of the stock market. The daily winning dollar amounts were simply determined by how many game entries occurred on that given day. There were hundreds, if not thousands of these daily numbers games occurring nationwide, all coordinated by organized crime.

The state-sanctioned lottery industry, the same ones who had shut down lotteries in the 1800s, saw the opportunity for revenue again, threw their arms up, and started offering numbers games as well. But the illegal games that were more frequent and easier to play, and winners could have their money delivered to their front doorstep (or maybe the back door) by hustling criminals. Early DoorDash for lottery winners…how convenient.

By the 1920s, illegal numbers games were thriving. Notorious gangsters were leading regional game systems, with well-known gangsters like Dutch Schultz running the New York racket and none other than Al Capone running the Chicago games. By this time, the numbers game went by several different monikers, such as the numbers racket, the Mafia lottery, the Italian lottery, or just the daily number.

Boston's reputation as a generally racist city wasn't helped by the crime syndicates running the numbers game there and they called the game the "n****r pool." This game was even labeled as such in the city newspapers because of its popularity among players in poorer, black neighborhoods of Boston and surrounding areas. We hear so many people talk about "the good old days" when referring to the 1940s and 1950s. They were not good.

In 1950, Jerry Angiulo became the Mafia don in Boston, setting up a plan where his runners would be rewarded with one free ticket for every three sold to the public. The term "runners" is exactly as it sounds. These people were the underlings in the Mafia who would run around the city and generate entries (cash) for the game. The opportunity for a free ticket was appealing, and the level of hustle from the runners accelerated. The numbers game in Boston flourished. In Howie Carr's book *Hitman: The Untold Story of Johnny Martorano*, Carr writes that The Boston American (newspaper) was actually able to stay in business partly because it published the daily number.

By the end of the '50s, the famed Winter Hill Gang had formed in Somerville, Massachusetts and by the 1970s, James "Whitey" Bulger was leading its charge, well on his way to becoming one of America's most infamous and well-known criminals. In December of 1994, Bulger went on the lam after his former FBI handler in Boston, John Connolly, tipped him off about an upcoming racketeering indictment against him. Somehow Bulger managed to remain free of authorities for the next 16 years, living in somewhat plain sight in California until 2011. After his arrest, he was put on trial for 32 counts of racketeering, money laundering, extortion and weapons charges, not to mention complicity in nineteen murders. He was sentenced to two consecutive life sentences plus five years.

What very few remember about Bulger was that he "won" the lottery.

In the summer of 1991, Bulger and some associates possessed a winning Mass Millions lottery ticket. This ticket was purchased in Massachusetts at a store Bulger owned. The shared prize totaled $14 million and many people immediately smelled that something wasn't right. Nonetheless, Bulger continued collecting winnings annually, even when he was on the lam. Here's an entertaining excerpt from a 2020 book called *Hunting Whitey: The Inside Story of the Capture & Killing of America's Most Wanted Crime Boss.*[44]

> *Whitey's other siblings weren't talking about their fugitive brother's whereabouts in the months after he fled Boston. But just because they weren't talking didn't mean that they were immune from scrutiny.*
>
> *[Boston FBI Agent John] Gamel figured that if he couldn't find Bulger, he could at least inflict pain on him from afar. Gamel huddled with then–U.S. Attorney Donald K. Stern on an idea to seize Whitey's portion of a $14.3 million lottery jackpot he'd claimed back in 1991.*
>
> *The lottery win had been another one of Bulger's brilliant schemes to launder his drug, extortion, and loan-sharking money. Back in the summer of 1991, a winning Mass Millions lottery ticket had been purchased at the South Boston Liquor Mart by Michael Linskey, who was the brother of a Bulger underling named Patrick Linskey. The FBI had learned that once Whitey heard about the jackpot, he ordered the real winner to sign the ticket over, with Whitey and two associates paying $2.3 million cash for 50 percent of the winnings. Bulger himself paid Michael Linskey $700,000. Although Linskey lost money in the deal, he really had no choice. It came down to selling the ticket or risking his life. Kevin Weeks, whose name also appeared on the winning ticket, later claimed that Linskey had purchased a large batch of tickets to hand out as Christmas gifts and promised to split any winnings with Bulger and Weeks. But Weeks story makes little sense; the*

---

[44] Hunting Whitey: The Inside Story of the Capture & Killing of America's Most Wanted Crime Boss, Casey Sherman and Dave Wedge.

so-called Christmas gifts were purchased during the dog days of summer.

The gang took the winning ticket over to the South Boston Savings Bank, where they received a lottery check split four ways among the Linskey brothers, Bulger, and Weeks. The scam set up a twenty-year legitimate income stream for Whitey, where he earned $119,000 each year.

Lottery officials took some heat, but they too called Whitey's lotto win legitimate. "The only person that probably would have caused more trouble is if my mother had won," Massachusetts treasurer Joe Malone said at the time.

There was still $1.6 million left for Bulger to claim in 1995, so John Gamel won approval from the US Attorney to serve the Massachusetts State Lottery with a federal seizure warrant to confiscate the remainder of his winnings. The forfeiture suit would require Whitey Bulger to appear in court in thirty days or give up any rights to his lottery prize, which was scheduled to be paid out until 2010.

There was a lot of money on the table, and Gamel relished the fact that he'd just scored one for the good guys and might possibly smoke Whitey out from hiding. The runaway mobster didn't show up to court the next month, but his older sister did. Jean Holland came forward and demanded that she be made receiver of her brother's estate in his absence.

When Gamel first heard that Whitey's sister wanted to lay claim to his lottery money, he drove to her house and tried to interview her on the front porch.

"I want you to understand what it means to harbor a fugitive," he told her. "If you are knowingly harboring your brother in any way, we can lock you up for a full year."

> *Holland looked at the agent with utter contempt. She said nothing and disappeared through her front door. Soon after, her attorney called Gamel in his office and berated him for "intimidating" his client.*
>
> *Gamel locked eyes with Whitey's sister once again when she arrived at the Norfolk Superior Courthouse in Dedham, Massachusetts. Cameras packed the courthouse as Holland filed her claim to Whitey's winnings, stating that her brother had disappeared and that she had no idea where he was. Holland was treating her brother as if he were a missing person instead of the fugitive from justice that he truly was. The fight between Whitey Bulger's sister and the US government would be tied up in court for the next several years. Ultimately, the Bulger family wouldn't receive a penny from the lottery winnings.*

This is a common practice for organized crime and lotteries; members would contact lottery winners and offer to buy the winning ticket. The winner agrees, as the offer was sometimes incentivized with a bit more money than the winning amount. The criminal secures a clean winning lottery ticket, thus using that clean money. *Why wasn't this an episode of Ozark?*

And what of the illegal numbers game? By 2005, the Encyclopedia indicates that the black-market numbers game is still very much active in the U.S.A., often operating out of official businesses such as bars and other small retail stores. Officials in Charleston, South Carolina say that they estimate the illegal daily numbers game generates an average of $60,000 per day and that the organized crime leaders have streamlined the business; they just use the same winning numbers as the sanctioned state lottery winning numbers.

State-sanctioned numbers games still exist today as well. States typically take 50% of the pot, whereas the illegal games generally take 20 to 40%.

Another curious entry in the history of organized crime and lotteries is bolita. This game first hit the U.S. in Tampa, FL, a city that had experienced significant growth in the first half of the 1900s, growing from 15,839 people to 124,681 by 1950. That kind of population growth was transformative in many ways, and brought organized crime along with it. Much like Florida today, the Tampa of that era had a fair amount of different ethnic groups driving some of that population growth. According to a 2000 study[45] done out of the University of South Florida by Pam Iorio, Cubans, Spanish, and Italian immigrants drove a robust cigar industry in the Tampa area that brought money and visibility to the mid-coast area, further bolstered by the combination of ports and emerging railroads.

Bolita originated in Cuba and was introduced to the Tampa area in the mid-1890s. It is a simple game where participants pick a number from 1 to 100. Wooden balls (also numbered 1 to 100) would be put into a bag and tossed around a gathering of men. Several of the crowd would try to grab the bag as it was tossed into the air, and one person would eventually come up gripping a single ball from the still-closed bag. Upon cutting the bag open, the ball, still being gripped, would be declared the winning number. If anyone in the crowd had the winning number, they would be paid at a rate of eight times what that person paid in. Minimum bets were five cents and maximums were set by whoever was running the game. This a daily occurrence pulled in would-be winners

---

[45] Iorio, Pam (2000) "Political Excess Shaped by a Game of Chance: Tampa, bolita, and the First Half of the Twentieth Century," Sunland Tribune: Vol. 26 , Article 5. Available at: https://digitalcommons.usf.edu/sunlandtribune/vol26/iss1/5

every day at 9pm and twice on Sunday. It was also illegal. And very popular. People of all ethnicities and financial statuses across Tampa wanted in. But it wasn't until Charlie Wall got involved that things got really interesting.

According to Iorio's report, Wall was born in 1880, and his father, John, was the one-time mayor of Tampa. His mother came from a prominent and well-to-do Tampa family. In the span of two years, Wall's mother died, then his father also passed. That left Charlie Wall to be cared for by his stepmother, whose level of abuse of the orphan was significant enough (from Charlie's perspective) that he eventually shot and killed her. The result of that event was a short stint in jail and then Wall being shipped off to military school by his uncle, his new caretaker. Charlie was eventually expelled from school for visiting a brothel. It was at this point that Charlie transitioned to a life that stitched together gambling, crime, and politics in a way that deserves its own book.

Charlie made his inroads in gambling as a runner for horse track racing bets. The commissions he made gave him a taste for two things: cash and the value of establishing connections in high places. He correctly sensed that drawing a direct line between bolita and the powerful people of Tampa could very well equal money and power. Backroom deals, nepotism, and power-elite were a dynamic in every busy city in America. Why would Tampa be any different? Wall saw his chance.

Wall began by shielding bolita operators from the police. For a nice fee, of course. From there, Wall's used his street smarts to take that money and use it to influence voting and elections. Iorio's report says:

> Election day revealed an unruly and unsophisticated facet of this diverse community, a side at odds with the progressive and vibrant image city leaders so desperately wanted to portray. But the history of

Tampa contains an interesting sidebar: the men who ruled the city through most of the twentieth century were willing to put up with the city's wild elections and notorious gambling reputation, as long as they remained in power.

According to the Tampa Bay Times[46], by 1927, there were 300 bolita games running in illegal casinos, in the backrooms of legal businesses, and the living rooms of a smattering of private homes. There was plenty of opportunity in the city to buy numbers, even at City Hall itself. There were plenty of questionable outcomes and cheating as well. One way game runners cheated was to pick a number and freeze the ball; this makes it identifiable by touch through the thin fabric of the bag. They always chose a less-popular number for obvious reasons: If a high number of players placed a bet on ball No. 10, for example, the person running the bolita game wouldn't want that number pulled to avoid multiple high payouts and lower profit.

Charlie Wall's reputation and power continued to grow unabated, backed by an important bloc of residents in Ybor City, located in the 4th ward of Tampa. Politicians were hip to the fact that backing from Wall would win them elections and Wall leveraged that with local authorities and police to let the bolita operators continue with their illegal fund raising.

Iorio's report, quite a fun and interesting read, further expands on how gambling, bolita, payoffs, and election tampering went on for decades. "Many observers staunchly believe that during these decades [the 1920s through the 1940s], there was not a single honest election in Tampa/Hillsborough County." And Charlie Wall was right there in the middle of most of it.

---

[46] https://www.tampabay.com/life-culture/history/2021/09/28/bolita-tampas-illegal-lottery-was-deadly-and-lucrative/

Wall, entrenched in election fraud and violence was now a rousing success, generating wads of cash and keeping his cronies in power. Iorio's report refers to one of the bolita game operators raking in $57,000 in a single night. Wall's portion of that cash was 50%, which he used to continue gaining power and influence. Vicious cycle.

Election tampering had become so prominent in Tampa that the National Guard was brought in to maintain order for the 1935 mayoral election, giving the city a national reputation of being crooked. The following year brought about new voting technology, which made it more difficult to stuff paper ballot boxes. It also brought other power and money-hungry gangsters into the Tampa region. Which meant Wall had a target on his back, dodging an assassination attempt and other threats of violence over the next three years.

After a close crony of Wall's was killed by gangsters in 1938, Wall adeptly saw the writing on the wall (in blood, likely) and went to the Grand Jury to spill the details of his involvement in the bolita games and the connection to politics and elections. He fessed up, didn't name any names, and was released. He took off to Miami and a new set of Italian gangsters took over management of the bolita games. From 1940 to 1950, even with Wall out of the picture, the merry-go-round of bolita, payoffs, violence, and election fraud continued. Everyone was on the take. It would eventually take hearings at the United States Senate level to address the copious amounts of criminal activity in Tampa. An aging Wall testified again during the hearings. Iorio's report closes out the bolita story in Tampa with the following:

> The close relationship between gambling and politics was part of Tampa's culture. The 1950s saw the fading of this relationship, and symbolic of the demise of bolita's grip on Tampa was the violent

murder of Charlie Wall. On the evening of April 18, 1955, Wall was found in his bedroom with his throat slashed and his head smashed. The murderer was never apprehended. The brutal killing made front-page headlines. Although Wall had been inactive in Tampa gambling for many years, many assumed that this was an old score that had to be settled, the kind of end that occurs to someone who spends his life engaged in illegal activity. The death of Charlie Wall seemed to some to be a fitting end to this "black sheep" of a prominent family who found a way to use his connections, brains and organizational skills to create an illegal empire that not only defined Tampa for much of the twentieth century, but also defined the political dynamics of the city.

And it partly started with a neighborhood lottery.

Lottery crimes have occurred from within the governing bodies as well. If you recall, MUSL, based in Iowa, coordinates Powerball and has 38 U.S. state lottery systems as its members. They are not immune to corruption and abuse of power.

Eddie Tipton joined MUSL in 2003 as the director of information security, responsible for ensuring the security of the random number generators used in lotteries across multiple states. Tipton had expertise in programming and cryptography, which vaulted him to a respectable position at MUSL in a short amount of time.

The scandal involving Tipton began in 2010 when a surveillance camera captured him purchasing a lottery ticket at a gas station in Des Moines, Iowa. The ticket ended up being the winning ticket for a $16.5 million jackpot in the Hot Lotto game. Tipton initially claimed that he was not the winner, but the Iowa Lottery became suspicious and launched an investigation.

The investigation revealed that Tipton had rigged the system by programming the random number generator to produce certain winning numbers on specific days. He used this knowledge to purchase winning tickets, then enlisted the help of his brother, Tommy, and a friend, Robert Rhodes, to claim the prize money on his behalf. The trio set up a corporation called Hexham Investments to claim the winnings, but they failed to remain anonymous. Kurt Panouses would have been really disappointed. As a result of the slip in anonymity, the Iowa Lottery identified the winners.

Tipton was eventually arrested, charged with fraud, and sentenced to 25 years in prison. He was also forced to pay restitution in the amount of $2.2 million to the lottery. Tipton's brother, Tommy, and friend, Robert Rhodes, were also charged and sentenced to prison.

The scandal involving Tipton had a significant impact on the lottery industry. It exposed weaknesses in the security of random number generators and highlighted the potential for fraud in the system. The scandal led to much tighter regulation and scrutiny of the industry, as well as the introduction of new security measures to prevent similar incidents from happening in the future.

One of the most significant changes introduced after the scandal was the requirement for lottery officials to undergo background checks. Prior to the scandal—get ready for this—background checks were not required for lottery employees. How background checks for lottery employees were not required before 2017 is rather stunning in its complete lack of foresight.

The Tipton scandal also led to changes in the way random number generators are tested and certified. Prior to the scandal, it was by the manufacturers themselves, which led to potential conflicts of interest. Following the scandal, independent testing and certification became mandatory for all number generators used in lotteries.

The scandal also led to increased public skepticism of lotteries and the fairness of the system. Many people questioned the legitimacy of the lottery and speculation grew about other cheating employees. Regardless, the allure of winning has clearly trumped any lack of trust as people continue to spend, spend, and spend some more on the lottery. Lottery officials arguably did not have to put too much blood, sweat, and tears into restoring confidence in the system.

By the way, Tipton served five years in prison and was granted parole in January of 2022, only to see his parole revoked soon after getting into some trouble in prison just before his scheduled release. Ouch.

MUSL's chief executive at the time was Charles Strutt, who helmed MUSL from its inception in 1987 and served for 28 years. While there isn't any evidence that Strutt was involved in Tipton's wrongdoings, he was removed from his position in December 2015. Merry Christmas. Strutt didn't leave empty-handed, though. His voluntary termination agreement contained a $284,000 severance payment, probably paid for by all of us lottery losers.

CHAPTER NINE

Charlie

Massachusetts has many small towns steeped in history. In one part of the state, there is a small town we'll call Northam, located northwest of Boston. The 12-square-mile town has been around the block, having been incorporated in the 1600's. Like a lot of early-established New England towns, it was predominantly set up for farming. Today, Northam remains almost entirely residential, though some small businesses have made their way into the town over the past 25 years. Traffic and bustle are not its hallmarks.

Down one of the main roads, you'll find a little bed and breakfast. Its owner and passionate historian is Charlie[47], now in his mid-fifties and a lifelong resident of Northam.

"I grew up in small-town America, 15th generation Northamite. I go right back to John Prescott and Thomas Sawyer. I love history and genealogy and I've been studying it since I was ten, so I know my roots pretty well."

"We lacked for nothing growing up. We were quite comfortable. We had fun vacations for 2 to 3 weeks a year at

---

[47] not his real name

the Cape or Martha's Vineyard or we'd go up to the White Mountains in New Hampshire. We'd regularly visit relatives, especially my mother's father and stepmother, my grandparents up in Northern New England for holidays."

Charlie also notes that his parents were pretty traditional when it came to playing the lottery. Most of the excitement during this time, the mid-to-late 1970s, was the Massachusetts Lottery's Big Money Game Show, which aired on local TV and was hosted by local radio personality Tom Russell. The Big Money Game Show aired on Wednesday nights, quite popular in the area. Charlie's father would even play. Charlie recalls hearing his parents talk about winning and how nice it would be to go on an extended vacation. Nobody had preconceived notions about retiring on it, as jackpots just weren't as large back then as they are now. It was more for fun than desperation.

"It wasn't like a big thing," he explains, "he might get tickets if he had a bonus at work. My mother couldn't care less. She didn't get into any of that, but my father would dabble a little. Nothing major. It would have been nice if we won!"

Despite Northam's general sleepiness, the socio-political women's movement in the 1970s certainly didn't skip over the town. The movement challenged traditional gender roles, and while the national TV news was focused on larger events —grassroots activism, rallies, and consciousness-raising in cities—the movement played out more quietly in living rooms across small-town United States. The dynamics of marriage roles in the 1970s were front-and-center, even in Northam.

"My mother wanted a career path, and my father did not want that at all. He had a well-paying job. My mother didn't need to work, but she studied nursing in college and wanted to get back into finishing her nursing degree. My father was a very old-school Yankee - pay your bills, don't live outside your means."

Charlie explains that his father's living was more by the book: living within his means, paying his bills on time, and having a well-organized home, whereas his mother took a more relaxed approach.

Charlie's sister Annie has her own perspective. "Whatever his reasons, he was not at all supportive of my mother working outside of the house or finishing her degree," she says. "My dad wanted a normal, boring, predictable life. My mom craved more excitement. She wanted to finish her nursing degree and go back to work. My dad even went to the college and demanded that they unenroll her because she was his wife.

"So anyways," Charlie explains ruefully, "she went into healthcare. He wasn't happy with that. The marriage fell apart for that and other reasons, and by the time I got to eighth grade, they divorced, sadly. And the world kind of crashed down around me when I was around 12 or 13."

The divorce bears some more detail, as it's quite relevant and shaped Charlie's life for many years to come. The court date to decide custody rights was pivotal, as it threw the entire family into a tailspin that still resonates with Charlie. The kids had been told prior to the custody ruling that the plan was for their father to live next door with his own mother while the rest of the kids would stay with their mother in the house they were already comfortable in, and accustomed to. Charlie preferred this plan.

Something went awry and Charlie's father was granted custody of the children, as the judge felt their father should have the house, seeing that it was on farmland given to him by his mother. The court also felt that it would be better for the kids to stay in the house they were living in and keep attending the schools they were in. Their mother simply had no alternative plan for where she would house them if she was granted custody. Suddenly, their mother moved out of the family home and in with, in Annie's words, "a new friend" that she had recently made.

"She never even considered losing custody of us as an option," Annie describes, "and as a bonus, my father was now replaced with an angry and bitter person, much angrier than before the divorce. I imagine things were worse for my brother. He was now being forced to live with the parent he specifically chose not to live with. I wasn't with him when he got the news. We both grew up in a hurry that day."

Both Charlie and Annie were placed into a counseling group at school and by all accounts, they were not complimentary of their father in those sessions. Unbeknownst to them, this feedback was getting back to their dad.

"This created a further rift between my father and brother because my brother was shining a light on my dad's treatment of him," explained Annie. "I believe that when we lost our family, my brother found parents in my grandparents and other families in the church. They welcomed him, and he grew close to many other families in the church. He went on to a religious boarding school and spent summers at the religious camp. He stayed very little at my dad's house in high school and mostly at my grandparents. My brother essentially became homeless when my parents divorced. My mom didn't want him, and my dad hated his religion and religious practices and therefore did not approve of him. My brother was a constant disappointment to my father, and my father was not quiet about his new thoughts on my brother. It was incredibly sad."

This short period of Charlie's life set the stage for the 35 years that followed.

Being the child of two very different people meant that Charlie was bound to pick up the financial habits of one or the other, right?

"I guess my nature financially was to be more like my father, but my reality was that I'd sometimes fall into my mother's category. I suppose that's an honest answer. You know, I'd pay bills, but I may be 30 days late on an electric bill or something now and then. Sometimes I felt like my father was paying bills before they even came," he says with a laugh, "but I wasn't looking to screw anybody out of their money or anything. So maybe I was somewhere in the middle? When times got really bad for me and I had little money, I would fall behind, it was embarrassing, and I didn't like it, but it was the reality of my circumstances at that time."

With virtually nowhere to go in the summer of 1996, Charlie became a caregiver for his grandfather's 85-year-old first cousin, Edith. She became like a great-grandmother to him. She and her sister took a liking to him. He moved in and slept on the pull-out couch. While holding down a full-time job at a local college, he shoveled snow after every storm, mowed the lawn, raked leaves, vacuumed, and took Edith to her doctor appointments.

Annie's observations about this period in Charlie's life hold some charm. "He grew close to Edith and Louise when he started his interest in genealogy around the age of 10. He spent endless hours with them learning about family history. This is not something your 'normal' boy of that age chose to do in their free time. He was always understood, appreciated, and accepted more by older adult relatives than by his peers and own parents. Edith and Louise also taught him to needlepoint. They were kindred spirits, and both were sassy and outspoken. They got along really well. His moving in with Edith made perfect sense to me."

As time marched on, Charlie's job at the college ran into some controversy. "I lost my job at the college, mainly due to personality clashes with the VP of Finance and the human resource manager as well as general internal campus politics. I was among a group who opposed a merger being proposed with a sister institution in Michigan. We prevailed at a constituency meeting, but several key supporters on campus made a point to get as many of us fired as possible during the course of the next year. I wasn't the only one to be booted."

When the job at the college ended, he re-entered the world of mortgage origination, something he had done part-time when he himself was in college. The mortgage business in the late '90s and early '00s was buzzing, so Charlie was able to subside and manage his own hours while working from home, which gave him the flexibility to continue to care for Edith. He added more caregiving to his plate, taking her to social activities such as her weekly Bingo games, visiting her family and friends, doing her grocery shopping, and other various engagements.

"As she got older, my assistance level increased, but I was happy to help her and glad to have a happy home to live in. She died in March of 2004, a few months shy of her 93rd birthday. I still miss her," he says.

When Edith passed away, it was clear that she appreciated his dedication to her well-being—she left him her house in the will. He now had a house of his own, and a part-time job doing mortgage origination, but was not on what most people would call a traditional path.

"I was always a bit unconventional," he says with a grin, "I had some nine-to-five jobs in the past, but I'm more of a maverick, a dreamer, and kind of a contrarian."

Annie fully supports that statement. "He was a total maverick. He didn't fit in easily from middle school on with his peers or my father. He was always a dreamer and had a great imagination and sense of curiosity. I believe he became a contrarian by necessity for the church, as he became a vegetarian and the religious beliefs of the church differed widely from the beliefs of society. I also wonder if he became a contrarian to stand up to my father and my father's beliefs which differed from his."

And now, Charlie found himself in a situation. He inherited a well-kept older home and a little money. "I had some money, about $100,000, and I was thinking about what I could do with this opportunity. I liked being a caregiver for her. I liked helping her and helping people. I'd worked as an orderly through college part-time at a local nursing home. So I thought to myself that I've got this large house. I've got a little over two acres of land, and I have this equity and a little money. If I build a large addition off the back with an elevator, I could create an assisted living facility and I could invest in myself for my future. So with a big loan, it would take me 20 or 30 years to pay it off. But when I got to retirement age, I'd probably have a million-dollar property and a business where I'd be comfortable helping people."

Charlie took out a large loan for $240,000 and used some money from some stocks and other inheritances. He was working on architectural drawings and talking to investors as well. But soon after the plans were starting to formulate, Edith's nephew (Charlie's cousin) challenged the will. This would throw all of Charlie's well-intentioned plans into a total tailspin.

Despite what Charlie describes as some questionable maneuvers where his cousin's attorney was quite friendly with the judge, Charlie won the case. But it took two years and cost Charlie a large amount of that nest egg. It was now 2006, and two years of fighting and legal fees forced him to start revamping his plan.

The debt built up and the money was near gone. With the

small amount he had left, Charlie struggled to pay the mortgage and the bills. He looked for alternate funding sources or partners to try to salvage his project.

Then the market crashed in 2008.

"I tried to find scenarios to rescue my situation," he explains, "but it turned out to be in vain."

There was no community of investors left to talk with, and what little equity Charlie had left needed to be used for basic sustenance. He turned to a last resort, filing for bankruptcy and subsequently losing the house to foreclosure. Charlie still carries some ill will toward the mortgage industry. For those who didn't experience this time in United States history, this was an era of robo-signings, document forgery, and plenty of corner-cutting. He decided to engage in yet another legal battle in 2009 to try and overturn the foreclosure.

"I fought that for ten years," he says, with a frustrated tone.

Charlie is not a person who gives up easily.

"It was a long battle. I went all the way to the Massachusetts Supreme Judicial Court on one issue and made case law that is still quoted today in briefs! Still, they ruled nice for me on one issue and the other areas were not so nice. And then they said they were going to make it prospective, not retrospective and with that, I wasn't going to even benefit from the decision, which was pretty chumpy of them. But my life was quite strained and stressed."

And so it went for ten years.

"I had a brain, and I had tenacity. I was just going to keep fighting these people. Most people cave and get run over. I was in a unique position to litigate back and I did have some nonprofit attorneys helping me. At times, I learned a lot. I got quite a crash course on all the ins and outs of the legal system. But at the end of the day, I lost."

During the course of those two legal battles, Charlie lost it all. He filed for bankruptcy several times, none of which carried through to the end. Being out of money and fairly familiar with the legal system, he tried to handle his last attempt at the bankruptcy process himself and admits that he fumbled some things a lawyer would have been able to handle. He was in dire straits.

"Anybody in the court system dealing with mortgage issues knew me. I was a pain and a thorn in their side. If they actually ruled by the law and the facts, I should have had a favorable outcome. I should have overturned the foreclosure and still owned the building with the original mortgage lien on it, but no, foreclosure. I found myself living hand-to-mouth and in rather desperate financial circumstances," he said.

And desperate people do desperate things, as was illustrated with James Hayes. Only Charlie didn't resort to drugs or robbing banks or anything illegal to put his financial life in order. He did do something that not many people would even think about; he started selling maps and atlases door-to-door, a salesman straight out of the 1950s. They weren't Rand McNally maps, brand new off the shelf, these were antique maps and old atlases mostly from the late 1800s. Definitely something that a collector or at least an appreciator of relics might enjoy having in their possession. Charlie, a historian and collector himself, had plenty in stock to sell. Some of them were not in the best condition, but most of the pages were in good shape. It didn't make him rich or necessarily comfortable. His best day saw him gross just under $1,000 in sales, but that was just once; the exception and not the rule. Most days, he'd take in $50 to $100. Paying bills was tough. While selling his treasured collection, he also gave away copies of *Keys to Happiness,* a series of Christian literature booklets.

"I was in survival mode, trying to overturn the house

ruling so I could get my property back, return the foreclosure and try to negotiate something to rebuild and still do the assisted living thing," he explained.

He hadn't lost the selfless will to take care of people, but he had to take care of himself. There's a pecking order in life's needs, and things like electricity, rent, and food usurped the lottery. But if Charlie had a good day selling maps, he'd pick up a scratch ticket or two and win small amounts of money here and there. He just couldn't spend irresponsibly due to his low income, so it was infrequent. But a little extra here and there from a winning scratch ticket was definitely appreciated.

Most of the time it was driving on fumes. He'd see what maps he had, group them into a certain area of the state, and take them to that area, navigating the shortest route possible to optimize gas.

"I'd grab the maps and put them in my junker clunker car and drive to a chosen neighborhood. Sometimes I knew I didn't have enough gas money to get back," he says. "I always figured if it came down to it, I'd be the guy sitting by the gas station asking someone for five or ten bucks to get home."

He says it never did come to that, but he recalls these being the very lowest days of his financial problems. Being a very religious person, he would pray each time that he would make enough in map sales to get home. In 2010, he had a decent day selling maps and purchased a $20 scratch ticket.

"I won a thousand bucks on the Billion Dollar Blockbuster. I was very happy. I had to go to one of the state lottery offices to cash it because it was over $600 in winnings, so I had to go in person to claim it. Praise the Lord, I won a thousand bucks. After taxes, I got about 950 bucks," he says. "They also told me that anyone who won between $1,000 and $10,000 on that particular scratch ticket was automatically enrolled into a bonus second-chance prize draw. But they weren't going to do the bonus prize draw until the ticket was 100% sold through."

Most scratch tickets have a lifespan of a few years, so Charlie didn't think much of it after his 2010 win and moved on with life. As it turned out, the Billion Dollar Blockbuster also happened to be one of the most successful scratch tickets in the state's history, because the Mass Lottery kept it running for nearly ten years. Roughly 44,000 other people won between $1,000 and $10,000 during the game's lifespan, so each of those winners was entered into that same second-chance drawing as Charlie.

In 2018, eight years after he won the $1,000, Charlie was still living day-to-day, renting an upstairs bedroom from an old friend who worked at a local college. He had no known phone number, no cell phone, and for the most part, no known address. Guess who was trying to get a hold of him on April 19, 2018? The Massachusetts State Lottery Commission.

Charlie laughs, "Yeah, they couldn't get a hold of me. My father was named Charlie, too. I'm Charlie. So somehow, they got his phone number. I loved my father. He loved me. But he disapproved of my lifestyle and he hated that I kept fighting for the house. He was embarrassed that I was trying to make caselaw with the banks and was always in court. Anyway, they called him and they quickly ascertained that he was not the right Charlie. But he gave them the number where I was staying."

It had not been an easy eight years for Charlie. "I had been staying with some older friends from the church and college that I had worked in; they let me have a room upstairs and I paid them $50 bucks in rent per week. I helped them a lot. I'd shovel the snow or till the garden and split their firewood and all that. I still sometimes do it today. So I was staying there with them and the Mass Lottery called them."

Charlie laughs at this point because Clay, the owner of the house, tended to be a bit gullible. Scammers and salespeople would call the house all the time and Charlie adds that Clay's wife was always cutting him off at the pass before he gave out his Social Security number and bank information.

When the Massachussets State Lottery called, Clay answered the phone. Unaware that Charlie was upstairs doing some work tied to his court case, Clay wrote down the caller's name and phone number. Shortly after, Charlie came downstairs and Clay informed him that a person named Christian Teja from the Massachusetts State Lottery had called. Charlie laughed and insisted that it was just another scam, like all the others Clay seemed to attract. Clay kept telling Charlie that Christian sounded like the real deal.

"I said, 'Clay, you say that about every call that comes in.'" On and on it went, like an Abbott and Costello routine for a few minutes, until Charlie decided to go upstairs and look up Christian Teja's name on the Mass Lottery website.

"Yeah, I looked up the lottery website on my laptop. Sure enough, Christian Teja was the public relations guy," says Charlie.

But it still wasn't enough for him to believe it. Contrarian, remember? Anybody can look up any state lottery website and see the names of lottery employees. Charlie got the phone number from Clay's note, then compared that number to the number he saw on the website. The first six numbers matched, but the last four did not. Charlie was still skeptical, but he was getting more curious now. For a moment, he allowed himself to think this just might be real.

"So I decided I was going to call the main number on the Mass Lottery website, ask for this guy Christian Teja, and see if he even knew who I was. This was probably three in the afternoon and I got some lady with a rough Marge Simpson voice," he laughs. "I asked for Christian Teja and she asked me who was calling and I said my name. As soon as I said that, it was just like somebody flipped a switch. Her voice even changed. She said, very nicely 'Oh, I'm so glad you called. He was hoping you might call back today.'"

Charlie suddenly felt like he was in the Twilight Zone.

"So I get very cerebral and stoic," he described. She transferred the call and he was on the phone with Teja, who asked him for his mother's maiden name and the last 4 digits of his social security number. Charlie gave both. The information verified, Teja then asked Charlie if it would be okay to add the chairman of the Mass Lottery to the call on speakerphone. Once the chairman was on the phone, he asked Charlie if he played the lottery.

"I answered that I played when the jackpot was big and also a scratch ticket now and then. Then he asked me if I remembered winning $1000 back in 2010 and cashing it in Worcester. Then he asked if I knew why he was calling and I said 'Did I win the bonus prize?'"

In our conversation, Charlie amusingly puts on a game show voice and imitates the chairman. "Charlie, you won the bonus prize!"

A few moments of silence passed as Charlie processed this bit of news.

"So I think he was waiting for me to jump up and down with Bob Barker on the Price Is Right, you know? But I was just solidly cerebral and thinking there's a joke here somewhere. Someone is playing a trick on me. Who do I know that knows people at the Mass Lottery? Or I'm thinking about if I missed a tax payment and now they're trying to corner me to arrest me for back taxes or something."

The commissioner broke the extended silence, "He asked me what I thought. I said if everything he's telling me is true, this is very good news."

Teja told him it was very real and an exciting, life-changing event. He also strongly recommended that Charlie speak to some financial advisors and attorneys and, sensing that Charlie still didn't quite believe him, Teja reiterated that this was all real. The commissioner informed Charlie that he had one year to come down to the office, show two forms of I.D., sign some papers, and collect his first check.

Then Teja announced the prize.

Charlie had won $1 million a year for the rest of his life.

It was fast becoming very real for him, but even then, he still wasn't 100% there.

Charlie explained to Teja that he had a friend from church who had recently lost $50,000 to a scammer and that his eye doctor had also been scammed.

"I said, for Nigerians, you sound a lot like Americans," deadpanned Charlie, referencing the commonly known email scam that started back in the '90s.

"They started laughing and said 'no, no, Charlie, we are who we say we are. You come down here, we're open until five today or come down here any time. You have one year to collect your money.'"

Teja then explained that this would be the only communication from the state commission. They were not going to mail him anything or call him again, and then Teja reminded him one more time that he had one year to claim it. The phone call ended.

After 12 years of battling in foreclosure courts, being a contrarian, selling maps door-to-door, being unable to afford a cell phone, and living on dimes and nickels, Charlie took a breath—the deep kind where you know things are finally going to be ok. He had won the lottery.

Or had he?

Charlie was still in disbelief. He went downstairs and told Clay the news. They both prayed. Minutes after hearing that he'd just won a million dollars a year for the rest of his life, Charlie prayed for wisdom and discernment that if this was a fraud or scam that God would protect him and help him not fall into a trap. He prayed that if it was real, that God would provide him the wisdom and guidance to know how to handle it. And of course, Charlie thanked God if it was true.

Ever suspicious, Charlie reached out to more state officials. Grace Ross, a local political activist, was well-known in Massachusetts as a two-time candidate for Governor. She was also a good resource for Charlie since he knew her through his years in foreclosure court cases. She knew seemed to know everyone, so he called her.

"I mentioned to her that I had a strange thing happening and I wasn't sure what to make of it and if was real or not," he says. Within hours, Grace Ross had called one of the lawyers who works with the Massachusetts Lottery. That lawyer called the lottery office and verified that it was the real deal. "I was the one that they picked. One in 40,000 or so odds."

It finally hit him. It was real.

His sister quipped, "That lucky bastard, he did it. He found a way to live his dream of being able to succeed without ever having to work 9 to 5. Nice."

The next steps were to decide what to do about anonymity. In a serendipitous turn of events, the neighboring state of New Hampshire had just ruled on a case a few months prior to Charlie's win, which allowed a woman who had won the lottery to remain anonymous due to concerns for her safety and financial well-being. Charlie's experiences with the courts over the years paid off for him, as he knew that state decisions of that caliber set precedents and influence in other states, especially neighboring ones.

Because of this ruling, Massachusetts started making provisions to accommodate lottery winners to set up trusts, and Charlie was allowed to have one set up. His name doesn't appear on it. The name of the trust is tied to the date he won, April 19. That date is significant for him as it is Patriots Day in Massachusetts, which Charlie describes as "the day my ancestors marched on Lexington and Concord and kicked British ass all the way back to Boston."

So he named his trust the Patriot's Day Miracle Nominee Trust, one of the very first set up for a lottery winner in Massachusetts. His lawyer handled all the photos, press, and media associated with his win. A month or so later, he collected his first check. By then, it seemed like everyone in Northam knew about it anyway. He suspected that his father would probably talk about it around town a little, and, even with an anonymous trust, local people knew.

"I got some anonymous cuckoo mail here and there, but people sending me strange things telling me they knew who I was…just weird stuff. I don't know what they thought they were achieving. It was a little creepy. I think my attorney has gotten a bunch of emails, but he screens it and doesn't even bother to talk about that irrelevant stuff with me."

During the month it took to set up the anonymous trust, Charlie had another decision to make: whether to take the cash in a lump sum payment over 20 years, or opt for the slightly riskier annuity of $1 million per year for life. Taking the lump sum would guarantee 20 years of payments to his trust if he dropped dead on day one. Also, taking the lump sum would have been based on a $20 million dollar payout, which means that after taxes and all, the lump sum one-time payout would have been in the neighborhood of $11 million. Charlie considered it, but knowing that he wasn't used to gigantic sums of money, he thought it might be a heck of a ride for maybe five years and then misery the rest of his life.

"But with the annuity, I could have quite a lot of fun. And if I screwed up, I got a redo every year. So I was 50 at the time, now I'm 55," he says, "and I plan to live a long time. I never smoke. I don't drink alcohol. I've been a vegetarian since I was 14. I'm a Seventh-day Adventist Christian, so I'm very health-conscious to begin with. I plan to live a good long time. They're going to regret me," he says with a chuckle. "I think I have another 50 years, maybe 'till I'm 105! I have plenty of tread on my tires."

So Charlie chose the annuity, as he's convinced he will live far longer than 20 years and since it's a million bucks for life, he thinks he'll live longer than 20 years and come out way ahead.

"After taxes and tithes, I walk away with about $600 thousand per year," he says.

I ask him about his tithing. Charlie explains, "I pay a 10% tithe to the Lord. I believe 10% of one's income belongs to the Lord and you're supposed to return that to him in whatever manner or guidance you feel is right."

Now it was time for Charlie to have some real fun, right? Well, not so much. Of course, after years of court battles and selling maps door-to-door, his life changed a little. But in listening to him speak about his life since winning the lottery, it is remarkable how much actually hasn't changed.

"Well, I still use my little Straight-Talk flip phone," he says, holding it up. That's right, he didn't even splurge on an iPhone or Samsung Galaxy. Or any smartphone, for that matter. He kept his flip phone. The same one he had before he won. And now, five years later, he still has it.

"I tell people 'smart me, dumb phone,'" he laughs at that.

Annie adds, "A lot of things are easier for him now, but my perception is that he's pretty much the same person and the money hasn't changed him much, if at all."

His largest purchase was, to no surprise, a property where he could continue to care for people. He purchased a bed-and-breakfast just months before COVID hit. Bad timing. So even as a lottery winner, bad luck kept hanging around.

"Yeah, I haven't been operating it since COVID," he says ruefully, "but I have a few longer-term people staying there and I've also done some renovation work because I figure that if I'm not going to run the business, I've got some deferred maintenance to catch up on. That should be wrapped up soon. So it's been good for write-offs!"

He talks about other bouts of spending, but not really at the level of a guy who just won a million bucks a year for life.

"I've had a couple of little sprees, just for fun, down to Plainridge," he says, referring to a casino south of Boston near the Rhode Island border. "One time I blew through five grand. I'm not proud to tell you that, but I'm being honest with you. I knew when I went there that I was blowing this money, but I'm embarrassed to say that because when I left there, I was thinking I could have used that money to help a lot of different people. So I don't do that regularly, to be sure."

He's also taken some close friends on a couple of vacations, one in particular to Europe. These are real friends, the ones who helped him out during his tough, financially-lean years. He's a person who simply enjoys giving back, which is another recurring theme throughout his life.

"There are always stories about lottery winners who buy mansions and shiny new sports cars. I am just not that guy," he says.

"I always said if I won the lottery, I'd still be driving a used vehicle. And still, to this day, I have never bought a brand-new vehicle. The first year I won, I still drove my crappy 1999 Toyota Camry around. The same little black Camry that I was driving around in selling maps. It was rusted out and horrible. I did buy a 2002 Ford Expedition after I won, but I got a good deal on it. It was older, but it had low mileage and was well cared for. I kept the Camry because my grandmother was in the nursing home, and I would take her to church on Sabbaths, she could not get in and out of the Expedition because it was so high up, so I kept the Camry."

Charlie did get rid of the Camry after his grandmother passed away, donating it to a local family in need.

It's clear in talking to Charlie that the money hasn't gone to his head. Not even close. It's made his life a bit easier, of course, but he ended up staying in the very same upstairs bedroom with his friends from the church for a full year following his win. The same place where the Massachussetts Lottery called to tell him he'd won. Charlie still gives those same friends some money each year. "Five grand here and there" he says and then adds, "It sure made me feel good to help them with some things they need. I help some of their grandchildren with some tuition at school, too."

Paying a kind deed forward.

Annie agrees. "Charlie is absolutely still Charlie. He is, though, a much better version of Charlie. I mean that in the sense that he is finally justified by disapproving family in doing what he wants to do. He has always been a generous person who likes to be around his people, including family, his self-made church family, and friends who just like him, dance to the beat of their own drums. He is no longer stressed about finances and he is able to be *more* generous. He is able to give back to all of the folks in his church family who took him into their fold. He is able to carry out religious work by helping those who need help. I think he is much more confident in who he is now. He has enough money to be free and can now live his best life."

After that first year, he was able to buy his grandfather's house in Northam. It's a modest house, roughly 1,700 square feet and he still lives there today.

"I honestly feel like the same person," he says, "I just have extra options now. As a Christian, I believe God expects us to be good stewards. I don't know how or why I came to be chosen for this generous turn of events. It's still very much surreal, but I do remember the hard times and I'm very sympathetic to those who are still stuck in hard times. There's a balancing act. I always want to say yes, but I can't. I can't fix all my problems. Lord knows I can't fix everybody else's either. So that's hard. I have a hard time sometimes having to say no to people."

Like a lot of lottery winners, Charlie had some things to learn. One of those lessons is saying no. Charlie lives a life of service to both God and his community, and one thing that has been tough for him is trying to figure out where the line is between charitable giving and being taken advantage of. A tough shoe to break in.

He told me a story about a fellow member of the church, an elderly man in his eighties who had lost two of his children. He was struggling and had lost most of his money. He went to Charlie and said he needed an exam and new glasses, but didn't have the $2,000 needed. Charlie said he would gladly help out when his annual check came in April. But this church member called him back in March, desperate for the money. Charlie agreed to help out and gave this man the money. Then something strange happened. He came back about a week later asking for more money. Charlie asked about the money he had gave him the prior week and the man said he had given it to another friend who needed it. A person online. You know where this is going, right? The person said he was from Nigeria and in the hospital.

Charlie explains more. "So this church member was very angry that I would not give him more money to help this Christian man in Nigeria. And he got very indignant with me. I thought, holy cow, I'm happy to help you but you're being scammed again. But he just wouldn't believe me. He would not believe that he was being scammed."

Charlie became more comfortable saying no after that. While the example with his friend from the church was an easy one to identify as a scam and say no to, there have been others since his win that were more difficult. It comes with the territory of winning—desperate people do desperate things.

"There's been some instances like that where I've learned to be a little more cautious and a little more investigative before I just hand somebody something. So I learned some things. I'm still learning things," he says.

He does make it a point to help whenever he can and in the right situation. So many people helped him during his hardships, and those are easy paybacks. Not always with money, but with service, or caregiving. He cites a friend whose wife died, and he didn't have the money to pay for her burial.

"He's a friend. I knew her, and he needed it," he says matter-of-factly, almost with a tone of obligation. He didn't hesitate to pay for it all. He gets a few other requests a couple of times per month, assesses them, and for some of them, he willingly and gladly helps out. He thinks all of the way back, even to childhood, about all the people who have helped him. Some people would help him financially here and there during high school, given his situation. He had help along the way, which he is clearly and eternally grateful for. For that reason, he is very happy to give back. He donates scholarship money to the local Christian academy—at least $15,000 a year to help kids in need. He helps with church projects, including one he's very proud of where members of his church took an international trip to help physically build a school.

"We were bending rebar in the sun," he says. "It was hot. We were lugging cement bags and sand and roofing materials, you name it." Not a typical lottery winner's endeavor!

"It's a joy to be able to give back. I also have to say I've learned where the balance is between God's prompting and ridiculousness when it comes to donating money. I find that sweet spot and try to be a good servant for the Lord and do right by what I've been given."

While it's a rare occasion when people win this kind of money, it's a good measurement of character to witness how a person changes - or doesn't change - when tremendous financial luck comes knocking. After winning $1 million per year for life, Charlie had every reason in the book to hit the gas on life and make up for more than a decade of financial dire straits. He easily could have spent lavishly on houses and cars. He could travel, frivolously and on a whim. He could invest every cent possible in an effort to make even more money. He could have all the new tech toys the day they come out. He could even choose to live near and associate with higher net-worth people. The money would allow him to be upper class—whatever that means these days —if he wanted to.

But he's obviously chosen a much different path. There is something in his DNA that has kept him grounded, humble, and even frugal. This is a guy who still uses his 2015 flip phone, lives in a well-worn 1700-square-foot house and has never purchased a new car. How many lottery winners of that dollar amount can say the same? There's no data on that, obviously, but it's not hard to guess.

Life has become much easier, but he still struggles as much with the everyday things people struggle with. He's never found a spouse and doesn't have a family.

"I'd sure like to find the right woman," he says, "but I've got to be careful there. I don't need a gold digger. I would sincerely love to find the right woman and have a family. It's on my priority list. And being a contrarian, I know I'm a hard sell," he laughs.

He also is very cognizant that he's no spring chicken. At 55, he knows he would have to find a significantly younger spouse if he's to have kids of his own, which is very much a goal for him. But he does maintain hope that it will happen in God's time.

"Yeah, that kind of a scenario, I don't want to marry just for family, but for true love. I'd be very happy. I'd welcome it. And I know it may not happen. I don't know," he pauses for a moment, then adds, "I'm not desperate, but I am motivated."

Overall, when I asked about his level of happiness, without hesitation he said, "Yeah! I was happy before I won, and I'm still happy. God is good! I have different things to be happy about and some things not to worry about anymore. I have new issues, like when I have to say no…that can be emotionally challenging and sad for me sometimes. But generally speaking, I'm the same person. And I have a different set of circumstances but I'm still me. I mean, I'm not perfect, but I'm trying to be a good Christian, a good steward, and a good citizen. I try to be a blessing, not a burden. It's still all a bit surreal."

It seems blessing, not burden, is certainly the more apt description of Charlie. Since his lottery win, he holds a weekly Friday night suppers at the Inn and invites many less-fortunate people from Northam and surrounding towns. He's bought a couple of antique cars, maybe a little bit for his own entertainment, but more because he likes to drive them during local parades to entertain local citizens. He makes it very clear that he got very good deals on all three cars and jumped right in to tell one particular story.

He was driving around one day and saw a great car. "I thought I'd get a picture of this car, so I pulled over and started to take some pictures," he said. "As I was taking pictures of this sweet, black and white 1955 Chevy Bel Air, the seller came out and started talking to me about how much it was, this and that. Well, before it was over, I heard myself making offers. They wanted $19,000 and I got him down to $17,500 and then he started telling me why he was selling it—his poor wife just went into a nursing home with Alzheimer's, and it was her favorite car. So he had to sell this car to put her in the nursing home. Until that moment, I was gonna try to get it down to $15,000 but then I said forget it, I'm stopping at $17,500. My empathy kicked in."

To drive the point home about his approach to finances, he adds, "But the value for that car is unlike a brand new car, where it drops like 20% right when you're off the lot. The Bel Air actually gets more valuable over time."

As we reached the end of our conversation, I asked him about defying the odds and whether he still plays the lottery.

"Oh, yes. I play a little more now, but I also didn't win to dump it all back in! I usually get one Mega Millions or one Powerball ticket per game. I'll do a quick pick. And there are some times when I lapse and I don't go any further. But now I'm buying my Powerball and my Mega Millions tickets in New Hampshire. I drive up Route 13 and go into Brookline, New Hampshire and I figure if I ever win, I will be moving to New Hampshire immediately, and before I cash them in, I'd be saying bye-bye Taxachusetts! They just passed that new stupid Communist tax where anything over a million for your income gets more taxed. So I would move to New Hampshire before I cash it, and it would be on a New Hampshire ticket. So I would save 9% in taxes. That's large money when you're talking hundreds of millions of dollars. I'd have my permanent residence up there fast."

In the meantime, Charlie continues to give. The Inn remains closed due to COVID and the unfinished building upgrades he's working on, but it remains a place to stay (at no cost, of course) for people who are down on their luck, like he was. Another quiet way, he says, for him to help out people close to him who are in need.

CHAPTER TEN
Problem Gambling

Interspersed within the chapters of this book are occasional light comments and sarcastic remarks about lotteries and the people who run them. This chapter will not have any of that. Why? Simply because gambling disorder, commonly referred to as compulsive gambling, problem gambling, or gambling addiction, is not funny.

Much like any other kind of compulsion, the level of damage that gambling disorder can inflict on someone's personal or professional life is significant. Stories of massive debt or personal loss don't just affect the gambler's daily and future well-being; they ripple like a heavy rock tossed into a lake. In the worst of cases, a person experiencing a gambling disorder runs a real risk of massive financial ruin, problems with the law, loss of job, estrangement from family, or even suicide. Here are some sobering points to know about gambling addiction:

- Gambling disorders affect about 1% of Americans, approximately 3.3 million people (Source: Yale

Medicine[48])

- As many as 750,000 young people, ages 14 to 21 have a gambling disorder (Source: Clinical & Research Institute on Addictions, University at Buffalo[49])
- Propensity for gambling disorder increases 23-fold for people with alcohol disorders (Source: National Institute of Alcohol Abuse and Alcoholism[50])

Money is an extraordinarily emotional thing. It's what dreams are made of. It is the thing that solves all of life's problems. It is what stands between doing whatever you want whenever you want, and not doing anything. Whatever house you want, whatever car you want, wherever you want it. Money is comfort. It is alluring. It is status. It changes everything. And there is no doubt that it makes parts of life better. But, after a certain level, happiness is not usually one of them—as many wealthy people can attest.

Gambling disorder is generally designated as an emotional problem that can have huge financial consequences. The emotional high from winning and the devastation of losing can trigger impactful dopamine hits to the brain. Some brains can only find fulfillment in the extreme sides of agony and defeat. The boring middle is not stimulating or fun for the gambling addict, as it may be for the casual gambler.

Compulsive gambling can be born from any single event or a combination of multiple experiences. Experts believe that genetics likely play a role. A person's general ability to deal with everyday stress, or observations and experiences in their upbringing can also be a factor. Feel free to place blame at the

---

[48] https://www.yalemedicine.org/conditions/gambling-disorder

[49] https://www.buffalo.edu/cria/news_events/es/es3.html

[50] https://pubs.niaaa.nih.gov/publications/arh26-2/143-150.htm

feet of a lottery commission, a casino, or a horse track. These types of organizations certainly (and obviously) don't help a person who is experiencing a gambling disorder. But they also don't create the disorder, the same way a drug dealer on the streets doesn't create the need for a drug user. Or the same way, a convenience store selling cigarettes doesn't create that need for a smoker.

Keith Whyte has been the Executive Director of the National Council on Problem Gambling (NCPG) for the last 25 years. He is the head honcho. The main man. He arguably knows more about gambling policy than anyone you'll ever meet. He was a staff-of-one when he started and the organization has grown to a staff of ten in 2023. His goal is not an easy one: change the way U.S. citizens think about problem gambling and the people with gambling problems.

Prior to his role at the NCPG, Whyte was the Director of Research for the American Gaming Association, where he had access to, and copies of, just about every study that had ever been published on problem gambling. Not that there was a lot out there to consume in the mid-1990s, but Whyte read them all, and his understanding runs deep.

In describing the general view of gambling addicts, Whyte says, "If they think about them at all, it's primarily a lot of shame and stigma. A lot of blame and a lot of misunderstanding about this disorder."

He adds that his lofty goal is to get more people to understand that the disorder of gambling problems are preventable and treatable. These problems have deep biological and genetic roots, and that, much like people with drug or alcohol problems, they can be rehabilitated. Rehabilitation is important to Whyte.

"I spend a fair amount of my time on advocacy and making sure there's a spigot of money for treatment and research," he says. "We work at the state and particularly the federal level to try to make sure there's funding for research and programs to prevent and treat gambling problems. At the state level, we kind of have to push back on these bills to legalize sports betting or to allow the lottery to go online if they don't have adequate responsible gaming protections in place."

In addition to research and awareness, the NCPG also runs the national gambling helpline, which is like 911. It's a place for people to turn to when there is nowhere else to go. The staff of ten aren't the ones who answer the calls, but they train the counselors and ensure that calls get to the right places.

Inside the NCPG there are also responsible gambling initiatives. Whyte describes this as the organization advocating for a seat at the table in every U.S. state to help determine things like how a lottery should sell tickets online and the best use of emerging technology. It is frightening to think about the ease of access to lottery tickets, for example, if a person doesn't even need to leave home anymore to do it.

"A lot of my job is trying to help mitigate gambling-related harm. So we're trying to help all stakeholders balance the costs and benefits of legalized gambling. There's also some general gambling policy work and there's some stuff that's specific to the lottery," explains Whyte.

His job is larger than just lottery-related gambling abuse, though. His objectives span the entire gambling industry: casinos, sports betting, lotteries, you name it. Whyte spends a fair amount of his time as a critic of state governments for not using the massive gobs of revenue to balance the costs of benefits.

"The state governments tend to only be concerned about the benefits, and you see that with the way they've operated lotteries over the past couple decades," says Whyte, "I mean, I get when a private company doesn't support responsible gaming because they're just looking to increase third-quarter revenue. There's less of an excuse when a state lottery commissioner who works for the people as an agent of state government isn't pushing forward on responsible gambling."

Turning toward the lottery, Whyte is critical in some ways, yet complementary in other ways. As is the case with everything, it's complicated. Whyte says that one of the biggest unwritten stories in the gambling industry today is the growth of responsible gambling within some state lotteries. This is an improvement. Whyte has been in the game a long time now and history has shown that state lottery commissions typically treat problem gambling with lip service, especially in the 1990s.

"Back then, most lottery directors would tell you that their products were not gambling," Whyte says, with a hint of incredulousness, "But that changed, and some of it was our advocacy. Some of it was the lotteries starting to accept that they're part of the gambling industry. But what I would say now is that in terms of when we compare lotteries to commercial casinos or horse racing, lotteries are now one of the most responsible segments there is. They're a vertical that's adopted responsible gambling more than most of the rest and I think that's been astounding progress."

He's happy to share that the NCPG can boast 20 state lottery commissions that are members of the National Council. And while that's slightly less than 50% of the total state lottery commissions in existence, it's also far greater than the percentage of membership in the organization for commercial casinos, racing, and other non-state-sanctioned forms of gambling.

"The state lotteries don't get enough credit because they tend to be state agencies," Whyte says, "and they don't have huge PR departments who push out how wonderful they are. So when you look at membership across the verticals—we're a membership-based NGO—we get no government funding, we are solely funded by membership contributions. We want the industry to be members, so it's important we are neutral."

In other words, Whyte has no reason not to tell it like it is. Lottery commissions are more engaged and active in the NCPG than pretty much all other gambling verticals and organizations. High praise, coming from the executive director of a national organization focused on problem gambling. But hold on. Whyte adds that even today when his organization does surveys, roughly 40% of U.S. citizens still don't even view the lottery as gambling. Clearly, there's more work to do.

Some of that work began in 2018 when leaders from Whyte's NCPG and leaders from NASPL got together. (Because you are now a lottery expert, you already know that NAPSL is the North American Association of State and Provincial Lotteries, the organization that provides information and benefits of the collective state lottery organizations in North America.) What came out of those sessions was an interesting new process called the Responsible Gambling Verification, or what is now known amongst lottery officials as the RGV. The process allows any U.S. Lottery commission to submit its responsible gambling plans to the NCPG. Whyte and the NCPG then hire third-party assessors to review these plans against one of the three RGV levels. The assessors then return their findings with the level the state qualifies for.

This is notable for a couple of reasons. First off, NASPL pays for the costs of administering the RGV assessment program, and they also pay for the third-party certification. Here's an example where state lottery commissions are ahead of the game compared to casinos, racing tracks, and the like. Second, NASPL is the first trade association in any gambling vertical that participates and helps to fund a responsible gambling plan that has been assessed by a national council as meeting a minimum standard.

However, a reminder that only 20 state commissions are members of the NCPG. Whyte's overall goal should not surprise anyone one bit.

"The goal is that every state lottery will be at the top sustaining level of the RGV's three levels. That's going to take a while. But no other gambling trade association in the industry has ever done this. Not the casinos, not the tribes, not the tracks. NASPL has put real money behind it because, obviously, it costs a lot to hire these assessors, and through the dues of their members, it pays the cost of each of those assessments. And yet they don't have any oversight because we want it to be very transparent. When industry money comes in, we need to make sure that this is not just a whitewashing campaign," Whyte says.

Getting an RGV ranking is not a formality or a cakewalk for the state lottery commissions and some state commissions who've submitted plans have failed. But state plans are now shared among NASPL members, which means that state commissions can look at other state plans that have successfully acquired an RGV ranking and adjust their own state plan accordingly. For example, the Vermont lottery may have failed on their first attempt, and may look at the Virginia lottery plan, which has a top ranking in the RGV. Vermont may then adjust its responsible gambling initiatives to match closer to Virginia's in order to gain that top rating.

"I mean, that's a real commitment," says Whyte, "and it's something we're super, super proud of—that we were able to implement that. And I think when you look at things like internet lottery sales, that's a big issue right now. Historically lotteries have been physical retail and cash-dominant. But in the states where they allow internet sales now, almost every one of those states has built their e-commerce platform to meet our best practice online standards for responsible gambling and they've also had us certify their operations."

It's clear that the work Whyte has done since 1998 has made real inroads with state lotteries and much less so with other gambling verticals, and it's also clear that the divide is right along the line between non-profits (state lottery) and for-profits (casinos, tracks, sports betting). Not for lack of effort, though. Whyte and the NCPG have been urging the casinos and sportsbooks to adopt these standards.

"For the RGV process, we all got together and agreed it was a good idea," says Whyte. "The Georgia legislature, for example, did not say that the lottery commission responsible gambling plan must be certified by the National Council of Problem Gambling, but the lottery elected to do it voluntarily. And now for online sales, they're again smart enough to align our brand with theirs, since iLottery is bound to be a little controversial. They have embraced our responsible gambling standards in a way that the DraftKings and FanDuel and the Caesars and the MGM's of the world haven't. I give the lottery industry a lot of credit for coming to the table with very specific, very actionable, very demonstrable, responsible gambling programs."

With states now emulating other highly-rated states and also starting to commit to being rated through the RGV process funded by NASPL, it is clear that Whyte's work isn't going unnoticed. But what does it take to get certified to the top level or any level of the RGV assessment? Whyte mentions seven prime categories that are considered for an overall responsible gambling plan submitted by a state lottery commission:

- Overall planning
- Retailer training
- Employee training

- Public education and awareness
- Product oversight
- Research
- Advertising
- Resources

Each of those areas is reviewed by the third-party assessors for adequate proficiency in that area. The areas above are rated on the following 4-step scale:

- 4: Exceeds standards required for verification
- 3: Meets standards required for verification
- 2: Some improvement is required to meet standards
- 1: Considerable improvement is required to meet standards

A state lottery commission is considered proficient when three out of the four assessors assign a score of three or higher for the area of focus. To achieve a formal verification standard, a state lottery must be labeled as proficient in six of the eight plan elements. Assessors are encouraged to submit comments explaining their scores, but are required to comment in the event they score any of the eight areas a 1 or 2.

Whyte believes that a strong, responsible state lottery commission would work to train retailers on responsible gambling. And that this ongoing training would have pre and post-testing to measure positive change (hopefully not negative change!). Some states don't do this, but an A-plus rating isn't required for all seven categories, as a state might be extremely strong in six other categories. Hence the three ratings tiers in the RGV system.

At the beginning of this book, there was a small statistic from a LendingTree study that showed residents of

Massachusetts spend the most per capita on the lottery at $805.30, and how that amount was virtually double that of the next state on the list. A person may wonder how such a huge delta in average per capita lottery spending between the #1 state (Massachusetts) and the #2 state (New York) compares to the Massachusetts RGV rating and if there is any correlation there. In other words, is there something that Massachusetts is doing in regard to responsible gambling that helps drive that per capita number so high? Is there any correlation at all between per capita spending and gambling addiction awareness?

"They're not a leader in responsible gambling," Whyte says of Massachusetts. He adds that they're somewhere in the middle of the RGV ratings and believes the state is doing "just okay" in some categories.

Whyte also adds that the NCPG has never seen responsible gambling efforts cause a decrease in sales. On the contrary, Whyte believes that it actually increases sales, though the evidence isn't overwhelming yet.

"If a person feels like a lottery cares and they feel like that money is going to good causes and not harming the community, then they may engage more and engage longer. That's the theory for responsible gambling across the industry in general. We would say to the lottery that this is a way to get ahead of a potential negative.

"And Massachusetts, I don't think the lottery itself is funding any research on responsible gambling. The state of Massachusetts itself is doing a lot of research," says Whyte. "It's a challenging state, quite frankly. Culture matters and there's a strong culture of lottery play in Massachusetts that is not seen in other states. I don't know what you would do to demonstrably change that culture of play there, I'm sure other lottery directors have tried. But no one's ever been able to do it. Nobody else sells like Massachusetts, it's such an outlier."

Some states have implemented great strategies and are working as advocates for the system. Others aren't quite as great. Where Massachusetts—the state with the highest per-capita lottery spending—is still in the middle of the pack on the RGV scale, some states are shining beacons for Whyte's organization. He cites both Connecticut and Indiana as two.

"Connecticut has some really strong programs," he says, "They utilized an initial international program called GameSense, where they're trying to help inform and educate their customers in a fun and engaging way. It's not about the heavy-handed problem-gambling approach—you need to have that—but you need also to be able to engage with players in a modern and fun way where they're having an informed conversation about making better choices."

Whyte is careful to note that the GameSense program also includes some good content that actually helps and teaches people when *not* to play the lottery. He believes that this program is well executed, strong, and actually contributes to higher sales for the state. GameSense is not proprietary to Connecticut, it's a UK-based responsible-gambling group and a trademark of British Columbia Lottery Corporation, which can be used under license by any state lottery commission in the U.S.A.

Whyte then points out that the Indiana lottery is doing some interesting work with financial literacy, an area where there is still a whole lot of opportunity and work to do for every state lottery commission. Indiana is taking a proactive role in education for winners, given the overwhelming evidence of the number of large-lottery prizes ending up not so great for the winner, like James Hayes.

"So Indiana, they do a little financial literacy thing, where they show winners how to protect themselves…anonymity and all that," Whyte explains. "But there's a bit in there about the fact that a person is much more likely to develop a gambling problem." He goes on to explain that there are lots of reasons a winner may develop a habit of playing. "There may be cognitive distortions that you were somehow luckier than others, or that you feel like you're too rich to ever run out of money," Whyte says. So the states need to do more than just giving winners some literacy lessons that include *potential* negative consequences. They also need to include the signs of problem gambling, and how to get help. And the program can't just be a single two-hour session. It needs to be ongoing.

Whyte says the NCPG strongly recommends that if a person wins a jackpot, they should stop gambling after that, as they are putting themselves at a high risk for a gambling problem. History shows that winnings are statistically more likely to go away and Whyte feels this winner-education initiative in Indiana is a good thing to continue to lean into and a good thing for other states to copy.

When I asked him about having state-mandated financial education for jackpot winners (the same question asked to Kurt Panouses and Jay Zagorsky earlier in the book about states *mandating* some kind of financial education for large jackpot winners), Whyte's response was different, and arguably more creative.

Whyte thinks a more productive way to accomplish jackpot education would be through financial incentives. For example, the lottery commission could withhold a percent of the winnings until the winner completes some financial literacy classes, or they could offer a small bonus on top of the total jackpot. This would give the winner a true incentive to complete some training. It's not a heavy-handed mandate, as it would be an option for the winner, but any percent of winners who can get more educated on managing a huge pile of cash is a big win. Whyte points to Kentucky as a progressive state in this area.

The state of Kentucky asks its retailers to take an online training module which includes some basic instructions on how to operate the lottery machines in stores and other retail tips and instructions. And while the module is optional for the retailer, there is a level of gamification to the process, as the retailer can earn a certain number of points tied to the commission it gets for selling a winning lottery ticket. While today, none of those points are really tied to financial literacy for players, Whyte believes this could be used as a pattern to provide another level of education for players and winners.

Perhaps the more stunning piece of information I got from Whyte is the lack of real demographic studies or surveys with regards to who tends to fall into the traps of gambling addiction. He is also disturbed by the lack of a unified national approach to educating children and teens on the dangers of gambling. He also believes that lotteries could contribute to reducing the amount of problem gambling.

Whyte laments, with vigor, how the NCPG has been unable to engage with any of the national groups that are doing any kind of work on this issue. The closest they've come is collaborating on a project with the National Endowment for Financial Education, which ended up as a series of guides for loved ones of problem gamblers, not gamblers themselves, would-be gamblers, or young people. There was a version of those guides for financial planners and treatment professionals as well, but the main work was for loved ones. Whyte's home state of Virginia is the only state to mandate problem-gambling education in their schools. While it's wonderful that something is being done, Whyte is concerned that it's not enough and that it's too late for many people.

"Gambling-addiction prevention-education is not systemic," Whyte says, "it's not routine. There are no turn-key curricula. In fact, sometimes, gambling is actually used as a positive example. In some classes, teachers encourage kids to play poker to learn strategy and bluffing. And we've got teachers using lottery examples to talk about the randomness of events. It could be preventative if done in the right way but frankly, most of it is not."

In terms of demographics, Whyte says that nobody is looking at this on a national level, there is no federal funding for problem gambling research, and there's really little national information available on who gambles here in the U.S.A. The NCPG has conducted some surveys on gambling attitudes and gambling behavior, but the survey samples have been fairly small and don't have enough power to really break it down in detail. What he does get from those surveys is that minority races and ethnicities are associated with higher rates of gambling problems. The NCPG has some theories as to why that might be and that they are more tied to socioeconomic factors and lack of access to health care (institutional racism) than literal race or ethnic background. But Whyte readily and honestly admits that there is a lot that we just don't know. The NCPG's survey and subsequent report that Whyte mentioned included this in their section on demographics:

> While various demographic factors have statistically significant relationships with a person's gambling activities, the magnitude of these relationships with overall gambling is relatively minor. Males are somewhat more likely to gamble than females (78% to 69%). Likewise, gambling by racial or ethnic origin ranges from a low of 64 percent past year participation for Native Americans to a high of 80 percent for people of Asian ancestry.
>
> Those who have less than a high school diploma

appear less likely to gamble than those with higher educational attainment, but that difference is only marginally statistically significant.

A similar pattern is seen in gambling by household income. The lowest annual household income group (less than $25,000) is less likely to gamble than those with higher incomes, but differences between groups with incomes over $25,000 are slight.

Gambling increases by age up through those between 45 and 54 years old, and then decreases steadily through those 75 and older. The gap between the age group most likely to gamble (45 to 54, 81%) and the group least likely to gamble (75 and older, 64%), while not trivial, is not sufficiently large to be of use when designing programs. In general, those designing programs for problem gambling treatment, prevention, and awareness must consider all demographic segments of the population.

Demographics, however, do vary significantly when it comes to what type of gambling people participate in. Not surprisingly, many of the greatest disparities occur with gender. In craps or dice games, horse or dog racing, sports betting (both traditional and fantasy), roulette, and online gambling, male gamblers outnumber female gamblers by at least two to one (Figure 3-8). The only activities in which female participation comes close to that of males are raffles, bingo, and the lottery. These disparities are also reflected in the fact that 61 percent of nongamblers are female.

Age is also a significant determinant of both gambling participation and the choice of activities. Nongamblers are older, on average, than the participants in any form of gambling with a median age of 49. Among gamblers, the oldest median age is found in lottery players (47), with the youngest median age (34) found among craps or dice, roulette, and fantasy sports players and those who play online.

Nongamblers also have the lowest household income, with a median annual income of approximately $42,000 (Figure 3-10). At the other extreme, those playing craps or other dice games, roulette, card games, fantasy sports, raffles, or horse or dog racing had average incomes $15,000/year higher than the nongamblers.

Educational attainment, on the other hand, bore no meaningful relationship with gambling participation, though it does play some role in the choice of gambling activities. The average level of education for nongamblers and all forms of gamblers alike was having some college or an associate degree.

There were a lot of allegations in the 1990s and early 2000s that state lottery marketing efforts were deliberately targeting poor and minority communities, and Whyte believes that some state commissions did indeed lean in that direction. In a sign of progress, he also believes that today it is happening to a lesser extent, given the lottery play has become more broad and diverse. He refers to replication studies, where lottery prevalence and other questions would be asked in a region. A few years later, the same questions would be asked in the same region. Those studies were generally big enough that differences between gambling verticals were statistically significant. The University of Massachusetts Amherst School of Public Health and Health Sciences has the ongoing SIEGMA project[51], measuring the Social and Economic

---

[51] https://www.umass.edu/seigma/reports

Impacts of Gambling in Massachusetts. The project is in its 10th year and funded by the Massachusetts Gaming Commission. Its goal is to "carry out a comprehensive, multi-year research project, believed to be the first of its kind, on the economic and social impacts of introducing casino gambling in Massachusetts…understanding the social and economic effects…and in making annual scientifically-based recommendations to the Legislature."

The study is focused on problem gambling and its social and economic effects and while the majority of the studies are tied to the introduction of casino gambling in the state and before-and-after effects, there are some interesting metrics contained in the report pertaining to the state with the highest per capita lottery spending in the country, such as the fact that 6.2 out of 10 people in Massachusetts choose to gamble. Perhaps Massachusetts deserves its own book.

Across the country, though, problem gambling remains a terrible affliction. And it's largely misunderstood and underfunded. One of the more misunderstood, or perhaps less-broadcast, pieces of the puzzle is the treatment for problem gambling. For some reason, the majority of people know that a lot of afflictions like anxiety, depression, or ADHD can be partially treated with medication and behavioral treatments. Alcoholism and drug abuse similarly, though mutual support groups seem to also play a big role. How do we know this? Well, we just do. It's not because we've been formally educated on it, it's more through mass exposure in the media—TV shows, documentaries, movies, or our own personal experiences. Alcoholism and drug abuse drive ratings. For some reason, problem gambling just doesn't have that…cache. It doesn't reach us through media like other maladies do.

Whyte points out that most state lottery commissions don't

do nearly a good enough job of devoting enough of their gambling revenue to actually make sure that treatment is available, affordable, and accessible. The level of support within a state's geography can also vary widely. He once again cites Massachusetts, where people have a good shot of finding a good therapist in Boston. But if you're out in the less-populated and lower-income western part of the state, it will be much tougher. Tack on the issue that many people don't have insurance, and even if they do, most private insurers do not reimburse for therapy or a diagnosis of gambling addiction. So, if the state you live in isn't devoting resources to problem gambling, available treatment is going to be hard to come by. Going back to the stigma that Whyte referred to at the beginning of the chapter, many people pay for problem-gambling services privately because they don't want anybody to know about it. It's a vicious cycle—stigma, socioeconomic status, availability of help. In this way, problem gambling is much like many addictions and maladies.

"This is especially galling for lottery states," says Whyte. "Texas, which sells something like $4 billion in lottery tickets each year, has about a 50% profit rate and doesn't put a single penny of it to preventing or treating gambling addiction. So Texas is one of the states where there are no public funds for problem gambling. And there are more lottery states than there are commercial casino states in that situation. The District of Columbia is another great example. So it's an Achilles heel for the industry. You know, that much money is coming in, but you can't you can't even give 1% or something. It's got to be better than zero."

I can hear Dawn Nettles cheer.

Whyte goes on, "When you look at problem gambling compared to alcoholism or opioids or anything else, gambling generates probably somewhere around $125 billion, including casinos and lotteries, tribes, tracks, all that. The states spent less than 100 million of that money on problem gambling programs. We take big chunks of tax revenue on alcohol and cigarettes and a huge part of that tax revenue goes back into anti-smoking programs and teach-your-kids plans and all that kind of stuff. Yet almost none of the lottery revenue goes back into problem gambling. Some of it is because these lotteries were created before responsible gambling was really a thing. It's a big Achilles heel for the lottery industry."

Basically, like so many things in life, it's complicated. Whyte has a deep appreciation for the evolution in participation from NASPL and state lotteries through the RGV tiered-rating system, especially when he sees the utter lack of participation from casinos and other non-lottery entities. But the stigma and the treatment for problem gambling remains grossly underfunded and largely ignored by the states. We can do so much better.

Toward the end of our conversation, I asked Keith Whyte the same question I asked the rest of my interviewees: Does he play the lottery?

He laughs at the question.

"Well, I'm at work, so I'm prohibited from gambling during working hours, obviously," he says. "But I do gamble recreationally on occasion. It's rare that I buy a lottery ticket, but it's not unheard of. It's more likely that if I'm on vacation somewhere, I might play roulette because that's the best odds I can get without thinking. I work in gambling all day, so I don't want to think about odds and counting cards or any of that. If I'm there at roulette, it's either red or black, I take my ten bucks and hope to win but expect to lose."

CHAPTER ELEVEN
AR Platinum

It's early evening on a Monday night, and the guy who brands himself ARPlatinum sits in his car, parked in the driveway of his in-law's home in the Houston, Texas metropolitan area. What's striking is that only after 5 or 10 minutes of conversation, it's clear that the narrow confines of the car cannot contain his infectious energy. It's actually hard to imagine him asleep. It feels like he should be doing this interview in a large field house or airplane hangar, where he can walk back and forth swiftly from end to end, carrying on two conversations at once, all while stretching and gesturing his arms to help get that bounding, non-stop energy out.

ARPlatinum is all hustle.

ARPlatinum is also a loser.

Week after week, year after year. A loser. But he may be the happiest, most gregarious, hardest-working loser you may ever meet.

Keep reading, we'll get there.

ARPlatinum (he prefers to use his handle and not his real name) is a 39-year-old who grew up in Humble, Texas, a suburb of Houston. While it's easy to imagine him coming out of the womb already walking, talking, and hustling, his upbringing was fairly normal. His grandparents from his father's side were hardcore Pentecostals, not abnormal for Texas. He remembers being sent home from church basketball as a very young man because he was wearing…shorts. In Texas. During the summer.

The other side of his family? Different story. His grandfather on his mother's side was a blackjack dealer who loved going to casinos. They would take AR to Vegas at the drop of a hat, starting just before he turned 15. It's not hard to figure out which end of the fulcrum appealed to him more—the Pentecostal lifestyle or casinos and lottery tickets.

"I think I went to Vegas five times before I was even 15," he says, "but I actually didn't go back again until all this started when I was probably like 28 or 29."

We're getting to the "all this" part.

"But I always had this forbidden love of gambling, Vegas slot machines, lottery tickets. My mother would buy a $1 ticket and a $2 ticket here or there, but she never did anything crazy. We'd get a couple of scratch tickets for Christmas in our stockings. But through the years, I probably never bought anything that was more than $10 bucks, ever."

But it was there all the time. The allure, the rush. The potential glory of that cash windfall.

One specific day in 2007, at the age of 23, set him on the path he remains on today.

"I was getting my oil changed, which is weird because I've always changed my own oil. Anyway, for some reason, I took my car to Walmart. And I was like, well, while I'm here, let me look around and I saw these baseball cards. Growing up, I loved baseball cards and always had this passion for sports cards, memorabilia…sports in general. So I saw these cards and I was like, well, let me buy 20 bucks worth."

After buying the baseball cards, he opened them to find a rare card that had been autographed by Negro League player,

Joe Scott. Upon doing some research, AR realized he held something in his hand that other people might pay for. Maybe even a lot.

"To this day," he says, "I attribute that moment to what I do for a living now. For whatever reason, I went to get my oil changed and I got this autographed card. I'm actually trying to buy it back now. I keep looking for it to pop up on eBay. I'm talking about the exact one, not another one like it. The exact one. It's kind of like that first dollar bill hanging up on the wall."

While researching the value of the card on the internet, he came across unboxing videos - dozens and dozens of videos of sports cards being unboxed and card packages opened.

"I see these people on YouTube doing these boring videos of unboxing baseball cards, and it was this dorky crap," he says with a laugh. "So I started doing videos and I just became obsessed. Next thing I know, I have the second-largest YouTube channel for unboxing sports cards."

The next step for AR was to find a way to monetize this new-found celebrity. Something more than just collecting some money from ad revenue on YouTube. To gamify the whole thing, he'd start by buying three boxes of basketball cards at $800 per box, an initial investment: $2,400. Then he would take a piece of paper and write down the top 24 teams in the league, lopping off the six worst teams. Through his now flourishing YouTube channel, he'd offer people the chance to buy into the 24 available spots at $100 per spot. Maybe you'd get chosen, maybe you wouldn't. The pool of people would be randomly chosen and then placed next to a team name. Given it was a random pool, sometimes the same person would have two teams. And then he'd open up the cards and perhaps the person might get a valuable rookie card. Or a Michael Jordan card. Or a Kevin Durant rookie card.

"People were so hyped up that for $100 bucks they might get a Michael Jordan card worth $2,000 and be able to pay their mortgage for two months," AR explains.

Or they would get nothing. So…it's a lottery.

"Yes. I marketed it as being cheaper than the boxes you'd buy at Walmart and you have way more chances to get really cool stuff. And it blew up. Next thing I know, I'm doing $20,000 a month in sports cards."

Remember, this is in 2007, right in the heart of an American financial crisis, and also at a time when the interest in sports cards had more or less been marginalized by the digital age. High-speed internet and instant access to action photos of any athlete at any time made sports cards passé. But not passé for everyone, clearly. AR makes the claim that he and a few others may have single-handedly saved the business of physical sports cards with this exercise. While there is no hard data to back up such a claim, it was certainly an interesting prospect.

"I'm buying boxes of cards for $800 each," AR says. "I was saying to people, hey, instead of spending 800 bucks on a box, let *me* buy the box and *you* spend $100. I'll even get rid of the six or eight teams that suck and you have a much better shot at getting a valuable card. But you also might get nothing. And it blew up! A lot other people started doing it, too, and now there's thousands and thousands of people that do this. They just had one at the Cowboy Stadium to celebrate Upper Deck! I'm not even a part of this sports card thing anymore, but I started it."

There was one problem, though. It was pretty much online gambling, and PayPal, AR's payment processor, was not a fan, given interstate gambling laws and all. Add to that the chargeback claims from frustrated people who didn't get picked for the sports card lottery and you have a problem brewing.

"I'm actually banned for life from PayPal now. I have some feelings about them, too," AR states, with a hint of disdain. He also finds it interesting that PayPal decided to put a stop to his account, but only after he'd run about $500,000 through the system and after PayPal had earned their 2.9% and 30 cents per transaction.

"Yeah, they weren't complaining back then," he adds.

The monetized game of chance that ARPlatinum had established with sports cards was over. AR went and found what he calls a real job, working in Sales and Management at a nationally-known gym. He managed the facility, normally comprised of a team of roughly 30 people, and it was during this time, twelve years at the chain, that AR picked up some extremely versatile skills that helped him get where he is today.

"I was cleaning toilets in the middle of the night in the beginning, though. I needed something because this whole YouTube thing with the sports cards wasn't working, and I had no PayPal account to do it. I had no way to take payments to keep buying baseball cards."

He eventually worked his way through the company. Sales, driving memberships, capital expenditures, managing budgets, repairs, maintenance, supplies, and managing people were all jobs he did while working for the gym. He says this job was pivotal to his success today.

"I learned a lot about people, a lot about corporate culture, and I think a lot of that trickles down to what I'm still doing today."

What he's doing today is a wild story and it's right on brand for AR.

About six years into his career at the gym, AR reached out to PayPal after noticing that there were plenty of people still doing sports card lotteries, and they all accepted PayPal. He expressed confusion why he was banned for doing it, but allowing others to continue.

"30 minutes later, I was reinstated," he said. But he had zero intention of getting back into the sports card side of it.

"I knew I wanted to avoid taking people's money for anything that could be considered gambling. I'm not an attorney, but now I knew there were weird interstate gambling laws and all sorts of things that could go wrong. I didn't want any part of it."

So halfway into his 12-year stint at the gym, AR was back in business. At what, he didn't know yet. But that would crystalize quickly.

"A lot of my success today came from the gym's corporate mission statement that we had to memorize and embrace," he says. "It was this culture that we were asked to exhibit at work. But come on, corporate lifestyles are never really implemented. The trickle-down never trickles down. The culture of caring and all that." AR says, mockingly.

"At the end of the day, it's the bottom line. I would go to these meetings and these seminars, and they'd fly people down here and I would have this and that on paper and the whole time I'm thinking how I can use this to implement something on YouTube? How can I grow my own business?"

At the same time, AR's boss was giving away lottery tickets to high-performing employees. AR played plenty of scratch tickets and he knew a bit about the lottery and the odds.

"I'd never played a $50 ticket before, and I was like, damn, this is crazy," he laughs, "because if you lose, that's a pair of shoes. That's a dinner I could have taken my wife out to. We could have gone to the movies. And then what if you go in and buy another one and lose on that, too? Now you're down $100. So I started doing research about what I could do to better my odds. I read through all kinds of lottery forums and found that so many of these forum posts have links to

YouTube."

What was initially AR's curiosity about bettering his odds of winning the lottery quickly pivoted to running a YouTube channel focused on the lottery and recording the actual process of buying tickets and scratching them off on camera. There were some channels already on YouTube doing this, but AR says they left a lot to be desired, and offered up his impression.

"Every single video was some person or other droning on and on and saying, 'um, so, um, like, um, um,' and the video was shaky. Just bad. And I was like, 'dude, come on man, I *want* to watch you, but I physically cannot get through this video you're trying to give to me. I can't do it.' And I had already been successful before in 2007 to 2010 with sports cards. So I said screw it. We'll see if I can do it again. If I can get 5,000 people to watch me open up baseball cards, I'm sure I can get more to watch me scratch off lottery tickets."

AR explains that this new endeavor was an effort for him to make a product that didn't exist in the market yet. Videos of someone scratching off lottery tickets, but in an entertaining way, with a professional-grade video production that was fun to watch.

The ARPlatinum channel launched on November 1st, 2015, with full branding. AR had wiped all of his prior internet history clean—social media, the prior YouTube content, everything. He was, in his words, trying to avoid "something stupid I said or did on video when I was drunk and 25." This time his approach was going to be almost Disney-esque - nothing at risk of suppression and purposefully made to reach a wider audience. The goal: make it entertaining as hell to watch someone win or lose on a scratch ticket.

"Everything I did was with purpose. I had this branding and I've had the exact same logo since November 1st, 2015. Same font, same branding, same everything for eight years now. And that was stuff that I picked up from the gym. My logo is black and white because I wanted people to see it and just know what it is. The other YouTube channels were all doing pictures of lottery tickets. But that social media profile picture is really just a little circle, that's all you get. People can't see a lottery ticket inside that circle, they go 'what the hell is this thing?'"

He still uses the same intros and outros from his first episode, and AR loves that there's a bit of mystique to it. People always ask him about his handle, ARPlatinum. He says it's really just his initials and platinum is an indicator of quality.

But it wasn't all smooth out of the gate. Despite the consistent branding, the big personality, and the voyeuristic allure of watching to see if someone wins big money, there were some learning cycles.

"Of course, the first two videos I put on the channel were in portrait mode," he laughs, "and everybody made fun of me. Other people got mad because I was scratching on what looked like a nice tablecloth. I don't think it was super nice, but people were writing to me that my wife was going to kill me for scratching on her nice tablecloth."

So AR dove even further into running a business on YouTube. He went through all the educational modules, the branding guidance, the quality advice, and whatever else he could get his mind around. Soon enough, he was producing quality videos every day.

"I had a one-year-old screaming, I had a wife who would come ask me questions and then I felt like a dick having to pause the video I'm recording and be like, 'guys, shut up, I'm working,'" he says, laughing again.

This was all happening while AR was still employed full-time at the gym, working 60+ hours a week. He lamented that he was taking more time away from people who already didn't get enough of his time—his family. It became a push-and-pull grind and AR's next step was to figure out a way to do it with less family interruption. Not because he found his family annoying but because he wanted to fast-track a way for his wife to see that there was real, long-term potential in his YouTube channel.

That problem would work itself out through some minor bumps in the road.

The gym was impressed enough with AR's success at his current location near Houston that they transferred him to a larger, more challenging, and struggling gym in Dallas.

"I moved to Dallas for them and I bonded with the General Manager there. She and I were going to turn that place around. It was going to be this great and wonderful business recovery story. A week later, they canned her and hired a new guy to be my boss and that didn't work out and I was let go. But they didn't want to pay to move me back to Houston, so now I had a house I was still paying for in Houston *and* an apartment in Dallas."

So AR figured he would just need to break his lease in Dallas to get back home. In the exit interview, the new boss mentioned they might be able to help financially, but AR refused, citing that he had now had about $7,000 a month coming in from his YouTube channel.

"And he goes from this lean-back position, sits up in his chair, and he goes, 'say that again?' and 'tell me more.' So an hour and a half later, the guy's freaking out," says AR, "because he's a sales guy above all, you know."

He remembers thinking in the exit interview about the frustration of it all—being moved to Dallas by a corporation, bonding with a trustworthy co-worker, only to have it all fall apart with a lack of support from corporate. And how in his interview, after being fired, the boss found this high level of respect for AR after hearing more about what he was doing on YouTube.

"I think that was kind of the beginning of the end at the gym because it kind of got out around the company down there about how much money I was making. Not to mention that this whole corporate culture thing was kind of frustrating."

So AR moved back to Houston and landed at another gym location in the area, but a 55 mile slog away from his house.

"My first day there, they knew. They knew about my channel, my silly little channel. So they've got all these lottery tickets on my office desk in my chair. They were like, 'we want you to feel welcome and we're so happy to have you here' and blah, blah, blah."

Three months later, management informed AR that they believed his lottery channel was getting in the way of work. He contended that he was doing much of his recording on weekends and said that he was able to put as much effort into the gym as he always had previously.

"But it had gotten out. I'm making a little more money," explains AR. "I think it started to rub the bosses the wrong way to know I was making the kind of money they were making. It just kind of went downhill from there. Then the pandemic hit and that was that."

The ARPlatinum channel kept on growing. AR, now back on PayPal, was simply selling AR-branded merchandise from the channel. He explains that if had wanted to, he could have accepted money from people all over the country, splitting the cost of lottery tickets and any subsequent winnings. This probably would have been very lucrative, but he opted not to, knowing that PayPal was fickle.

The branded merchandise being sold on the ARPlatinum store were custom-made coins that AR manufactured. These are the same coins he uses in his videos to scratch off the tickets he purchases. They're simple aluminum and AR laughs when talking about them because he receives frequent inquiries about why he's scratching off tickets in his videos with sobriety tokens. Alas, they are not sobriety tokens, they're just custom-made. AR believes no other coin scratches quite as well.

In watching the videos, you can see why.

"They are the perfect size, the perfect weight, and the perfect thickness," he says. "They scratch great. They come in all different colors, too."

He also offers seasonal-based or holiday-themed coins.

But it turns out that the story with PayPal wasn't quite over.

Selling coins through PayPal. Simple, right? Not gambling, just merch. Not offering anything else. Not so fast.

"One day I get an email, my account has been suspended so I call them immediately," he explains. "Whereas the last time I kind of knew I was doing stuff they didn't like, this time I had no idea why they suspended me. So I'm on the phone with them and they're eager to sort this out. I'm on hold and they come back and say there's nothing they can do. I asked to talk to a manager or something and they said I could have my attorney call them. I was like, what is going on? I've done nothing. I had about $1,500 sitting in my account and now it was going to be on hold for 180 days, because that's their policy. I was like, 'oh, this is lovely. Great.' It's not like I need this money or anything."

When AR went to PayPal 180 days later to follow up, his balance showed zero, and also showed a deduction of approximately $1,500 that had been in his account, for "damages caused." Upon reading PayPal's Terms of Service and End User Agreement, AR found that PayPal reserves the right to fine people $3,000 *per case per transaction.*

"This is part of their racket," he says. "So don't keep

money in PayPal. It's up to them to determine if you've violated their terms, and if they want to take your money, they can. And the alternative is you can take them to court and pay a bunch of attorney fees, which nobody's going to do. Then if they wanted to counter-sue me, even though I didn't do anything wrong, they could have fined me for the 1,000 transactions times $3,000. You're talking a $3 million countersuit? Nope. Take my $1,500. I'll just make sure to tell everyone not to use PayPal."

AR later found out that PayPal suspended the account due to an "elevated level of risk." Not much more was provided.

As of October 2023, the ARPlatinum channel on YouTube has produced over 5,000 videos and has 112,000 subscribers. The majority of the videos are simply of AR scratching tickets with his aluminum coins and losing more than he wins. He offers merchandise right through the YouTube channel, mostly apparel. He loses for a living. But does he?

"I track every dollar spent, and I publish it," he says. "I'm often behind, but I try to let people know the numbers every month and I keep a running balance. I did an interview with NPR a couple of weeks ago. In 2022, I spent $149,935 on scratch tickets and I got $116,695 back. So I lost $33,240 on the lottery, and that's probably close to a lot of people's median household income."

The key takeaway: his annual financial losses from the scratch tickets alone are made up (and then some) through advertising on his YouTube channel. He makes a full-time living off the channel, as many do. The scratch tickets are a loss leader!

His channel has gotten so popular that major casino brands are noticing, which means he has another stream of growing income as an internet influencer. He's very present on the Reddit lottery board and other internet lottery boards, and his posts are driving traffic to his YouTube channel, where he hooks users in with his well-produced, narrated, light, and fun-to-watch videos. He has found a clear niche, and nailed it.

He has turned losing in the lottery into winning. The rest of us are just doing the former.

"We're getting a million views or more per month now," he proudly says. "You can have a thousand subscribers and be monetized. You can make a little money with 1000 video views. But once you have one that just blows up and gets a million views, you're going to make $10 to $15 thousand on that one video alone."

And once one video goes viral like that, the ripple effect is very much in play and people will start watching other videos on the channel. The faucet is turned on. At 112,000 subscribers and counting, AR has created a legitimate and very interested community.

"I always want the videos to be in the first-person perspective to where, if they want, people can pause the video and play along. And if they want to just listen, they can just listen. Whatever it is. I just want this thing to be fun and I want to share some of the passion that I have for this with the people who are passionate about it," he says.

"It's funny," he reflects, "when I saw those $50 and $20 scratch tickets years ago, relative to my income, those felt insanely expensive. Now the amount of money I spend is stupid. It has really numbed me. I'll spend $3,000 in a single day on lottery tickets like it's nothing. And then I'll go to the grocery store and complain about a 12-pack of Mountain Dew costing me seven bucks. It's very strange how my brain sort of just cordons it off."

It baffles the mind how much AR has spent on scratch tickets over the course of eight years. Thousands of scratch tickets, hundreds of thousands of dollars spent. Somewhere in there along the way, there had to be a big winner, right? A

$10,000 win, maybe even a $50,000 windfall. AR is happy to answer this one.

"This is the most pathetic thing ever and a true testament to just how difficult it is to win the lottery. The most I've won is $1,000 on a ticket. Three times. In eight years."

Just let that sink in for a second.

AR has spent at least $100,000 every year on scratch tickets for about seven years, which is very likely more than what 99% of people spend. And he's won $1,000 three times. If that's not a testament that you're not going to win, then who knows what is?

"What makes you think you're going to be the one to win it?" asks AR. "It's not even in my head that I'm going to win big. I'm torn because people will give me shit for all this and tell me I'm part of the problem. But I try to discourage people from playing! Everybody always asks me what the best tickets are to play. I tell them 'none'. Save your money. Take your family out, dude. Just watch me, man! That's the whole point of the show, you know? I still have business cards from forever ago, where that was my slogan - watch me waste my money so you don't have to waste yours."

Unless he's a terrific actor, he really means it.

Ever gregarious and upbeat, this level of loss doesn't deter AR from making his videos. He even sort of gamified that, too.

"I came up with this brilliant marketing idea that I'm not going to cut my hair until I win a $1,000 pot," he said, clearly sarcastic when saying the word brilliant. "So fast-forward nine months, I still haven't won and now I've got this glorious mop. Then my sister was getting married and wanted me to be an usher. But then she called me a couple of days later and asked if wanted to do the ceremony. And now I'm a minister, I'm ordained! So I got ordained and I cut my hair because my dad was like, 'son, for God's sake, I only have one daughter.

It's your only sister. Will you cut this stupid hair and do this wedding ceremony?' So I cut my hair to do the ceremony and my subscribers were pissed. I cut my hair, but didn't win the $1,000. They said I don't stand by my word. I was like, 'it's my sister's wedding, come on!' But some of them were furious. So I grew it out again and it took another year to win the $1,000."

That $1,000 win came in October of 2021. Deftly, AR knew full well that YouTube ad rates rise significantly and sometimes even double during the October to December holiday season, so he sat on the video containing the $1,000 win until the end of the holiday season.

"Let me tell you, it was something else," he said. "Imagine me in corporate America with this giant hair."

* * *

AR, in all his afro glory (Photo courtesy of ARPlatinum)

The hustle isn't slowing down, either. AR tried to work with the Texas Lottery Commission on a behind-the-scenes set of videos. The video series was an idea for a how-it's-made type of project: the conception of tickets, the naming of games, price structure, payout structure, and what goes into determining anything and everything in a lottery commission. All of the behind-the-scenes stuff that most people don't know about and never see. He prepared a pitch for the commission and sent it off, initially getting a warm response and he was encouraged. They told him his audience hit their target demographic square on the nose. Then, suddenly, the commission went dark. AR explains what happened next.

"I got the most well-written rejection letter I've ever gotten," he said.

AR figured that since a state lottery commission is largely beholden to the state government, the government, or the Secretary of State or its attorneys probably wanted no part of that.

"I think they said 'there is no way you're going to let this guy infiltrate us.'"

This frustrated him a bit because he's passionate about his work and his integrity. Realizing that the commission felt threatened by him was puzzling.

"I don't publish how much money I make because then I feel like I will lose the everyman. I want my viewers all to feel like 'one of us.' I sometimes get the conspiracy theorists who think I work for the lottery commission. Now I'm like, bud, believe me, they want nothing to do with me. They made it perfectly clear."

In watching his videos, there is definitely an everyman vibe to them. His videos show repeated losses. And then more losses. Outside of his overwhelmingly positive tone, it's a pretty realistic portrayal of what happens when you spend money on scratch tickets. There are plenty of other lottery channels on YouTube that only show when people win.

"To me, those channels are misleading, especially when you consider the fact that most people—and I don't have the statistics—but I would venture to say a large majority of the people who play probably shouldn't be playing. They think scratch tickets are going to be the thing that gets them out of whatever situation they're in. It's not. The reality is it's the complete opposite. So you have these people who might not be as well educated as others already in a vulnerable state and desperate. They watch a YouTube lottery channel and just see winning, winning, winning? No. From an ethical standpoint, I show everything, wins and losses, even if it's to the detriment of views. My wins obviously get more views, get more ad revenue, and so on. But I just can't bring myself to only show when I win because I know what the end result of that is."

It's clear he feels some level of responsibility to not cater to or encourage the desperate. And yet, like many lottery winners, AR receives what he calls "an insane amount of people" who send emails or letters looking for money. But not all of them.

"Some of them will say they're going to die in 3 to 6 months, and my videos get them through terrible therapies and treatments. They want me to know I make a difference," he says, clearly touched by these notes.

But those aren't as common as the people who straight-up ask him for money. These requests show up daily, as predictable and reliable as the stifling summertime Texas heat. He's sure most are just scams, but AR is not one to fall victim to such things.

"I'll have people send me these sob stories and I tell everybody the same thing, which is that I can't give *you* money, and then tell the *next* person no. Because the next person will just tell everyone I'm an asshole, right? Or that I don't like a certain group of people. I didn't win the lottery! I have bills, I have a wife, I have a kid. We have to pay for college. But still, I get the people that flip out on me and start getting in the video comments and I end up having to block them. It's wild, the audacity some people have."

AR's profession is obviously not common. It is reliant on many things: continued viewership and interest from a fickle public, robust advertising rates that rise and fall with the economy, and a presumption that whatever the loss is on the lottery (and it will be a loss) is made up for through other revenue channels. It is not easy and it requires the hustle, smarts, time, and determination that AR has. At this point, I had to ask how his wife felt about his unconventional job.

"She's a registered nurse, so she's working, and I'm at home pretty much every day. At this point, she thinks it's funny because the entire purpose of all this was to make it financially successful based on what I learned from the gym," he says. "The first year I was in sales at the gym was awful, I think made $35,000. I was new to aggressive sales and it was not my thing. But the gym taught me a lot and I use sales tactics I learned then today. But with ten years of experience at the gym, I maxed out my base at like $65,000 a year. So yeah, she's good," he smiles, and then adds, "and I think she just gave up. She was like 'look dude, if this is what you're going to do, I can't stop it. So just try not to be an idiot, please.'"

It's here where AR turns—wait for it—a little philosophical regarding what his career change has meant for his life in general, getting emotional.

"I had to find a way to get my time back," he explains. "My dad was the CFO of an oil company, he's done that all his life. He was there for the big stuff. He never missed a game. He was there for us when we needed him. But other than that, he left the house at eight every morning and got home at ten every night, Monday to Friday."

He pauses for a second. "I make enough money to live my life. I can always go work more if I need to. I can go get another job. I can hustle. But I can't get my time back. Now I don't have to ask for PTO anymore. This has given me a hall pass to live my life. I have all of my time and I can put it where I want to. My wife loves that part. She doesn't want me to go back to traditional work because I can pick up our kid from school. I can be the baseball coach. I can do whatever."

He points out that there was a time at the gym, those years when he was working 50 to 60 hours per week and he was feeling bad because he felt like it wasn't enough. This is a work culture phenomenon that seems to only exist in America. In most other countries, a standard 40-hour work week is more than enough, not to mention the more generous vacation allowances. So AR working 50 to 60 hours per week and actually feeling bad about it for not giving them more is unique to the good old U.S.A., for the most part. Then he would get home and pick up his 3-month-old, who would then proceed to scream because he didn't know who AR was.

"That's when it dawned on me," he says, "I was making like 15 bucks an hour just to get out of the house, you know? And I was paying $800 a month for two days of childcare, and I realized, wow, I'm working 40 hours a week to make $1,600 a month after taxes and insurance, and I'm giving $800 of that to childcare, that's like $5 an hour. I was like 'good lord,' I can sell some merch or something and make $800 a month. So I did. I went down to one day a week at the gym, started selling these silly coins, and made more money. Then I got to spend more time with my kid. It was great."

You might not be too shocked to know that AR is not resting on his laurels. Up next for him is an impressive foray into what is essentially influencer marketing. When he's got the most popular lottery channel on YouTube, that gives him some capital, and he intends to use it.

He cemented a partnership with Caesars after "politely letting them know for two years how much I love them."

Persistence. Hustle. At first, they wanted no filming, no cameras, nothing. But through repeated efforts, he was able to break the egg with them, and he finally has another person working with him on filming and editing; an old friend from his gym days who went to film school and lost his job after the pandemic.

"I told him to follow me around because I'm doing this casino gig," he laughed. "I told him if he wanted to work on these big projects and build his resume, he should come with me. And the guy's amazing!"

He got his foot in the door with the Caesars Rewards program. They flew him and his wife in, put them up in a nice hotel for four nights, and told the pair to gamble like they normally would. Tough life!

"They just loved what we did," he beamed, "so we did it again in Reno and Tahoe, and then again in New Orleans."

In 2023, things will only get bigger. AR is helping create awareness for Caesars in rolling out a new offering called the Caesars Travel Bundle, where people can book their entire travel experience right through the Caesars website. They are now in partnership with airlines, hotels, car rental services, shows, dinner reservations, and various other things, all of it tied to a loyalty points system that presumably keeps customers loyal to Caesars the next time they plan something.

AR will also be involved in the grand opening of the Horseshoe, a Caesars re-branding of the old Bally's casino in Las Vegas.

"Yeah, we're going to do that and we're also going to do some shows and dinners at a couple of different places," he says. "We'll highlight the restaurants and the shows on my channel and just film the overall experience. I mean, my wife loves free trips to Vegas. Who doesn't, right? Who doesn't want to be flown all over the country? I'm getting paid to do things that people pay to do! But to be able to share that, not just with my fans and subscribers in my videos, but to also physically share the experience with my friends and my family, that's the best part."

He summarizes it all perfectly with this gem: "This whole thing has been a blessing, and it's the stupidest thing ever. It really is. And I don't try to hide that fact. People ask me 'wait, you do what?' And I tell them 'I basically scratch lottery tickets on film.' It's hilarious."

CHAPTER TWELVE

Epilogue

When I was around ten years old, I wrote a book that was a total rip-off of the 1980s hit TV show, The A-Team. It even had a similar van. I don't remember much about the book aside from it being pretty short, but I do remember the pride of telling the story and the satisfaction of completing it. It was written in pen, included drawings on 8x11 paper, and staples for a binding. So yeah, a book.

Since then, I've vowed to write a real book. Now, 41 years later, spurred on by external encouragement from a life-vision coach and others, here I am. What took me so long? Well, ideas came and went. Life got in the way. Despite continuing to write throughout my life, it never came together. I majored in Journalism & Mass Communication in college, did some writing for the school newspaper, and took film scriptwriting classes. I wrote features and music reviews for various publications and websites in the '90s. I kept a blog for about 15 years in the oughts and 2010s. But I always had a day job —I still do—that seemed to take up all of my time.

This book was written on nights and weekends mostly from November 2022 through March 2023, probably much to the dismay of my wife and two teenage sons, who during this time only saw me crouched over my laptop, obsessively clicking away on the keyboard, oblivious to nearly anything and everything around me. Many thanks to them for their patience, love, support, and understanding. I'm a lucky guy.

As a rookie author, I came into some beginner's luck of my own in finding a copy editor named Chandi Lyn. She was not only a total pro at shaping my writing, asking questions, and pushing back, but was also very fun and engaging to work with. Chandi led me down the path to Graeme Thomas Rosen, the proofreader who put the finishing touches on this book. His friendly demeanor and generous compliments actually made me blush a little, and certainly helped my ego. A heartfelt and deep thanks to both. This is just the beginning.

One last thanks to Theresa Garvin, for inspiring me to finally just put this in my vision and do it. This book wouldn't exist without her guidance.

My favorite story about this time is finally telling my parents that I was nearly done with a book. Although I didn't know what to expect with their reaction, I thought it might be a combination of exuberant pride, celebration, or excitement. Or all of those things at once. But upon telling them the news, my Dad, in his always-friendly and slightly sarcastic way, said "Finally."

Yeah, finally.

I've never been much of a lottery player. Like a lot of the people you met in this book, as an adult I have played very casually, and mostly when the jackpot goes over $500 million. As a child growing up in Massachusetts, I'm old enough to remember a couple of things lottery-related.

First, the launch of Megabucks, an early version of what we all know today as a Powerball-type game. It generated quite a bit of hype, as it promised jackpots the size which we'd not seen before. I remember going to the store with my parents during my middle school years and they gave me a Megabucks sheet, allowing me to pick a set of numbers. I studied it and circled a few. Later that night, I hit on three of those numbers and I think I won something like $20. I was spellbound. Thrilled! I probably spent that money on hockey cards and Fun Dip, but it wasn't until many years later that I thought back on that moment as a potentially pivotal moment where I could have spiraled into a lottery fiend or potentially even problem gambler. It was the first time I'd played a lottery game and my still-forming brain could have really latched on that dopamine hit. I'm so glad it didn't.

Second, the lottery in my house as a child was a fairly big deal. More for my mother than my father. I'd often get into my mom's car and see relatively large collections of discarded scratch tickets in the glove box or on the passenger-side floor. I remember more than once thinking what an enormous waste of money it seemed to be, but it was also never totally out of control or anything. She did it for fun, for the spot-on elation of winning, like most people.

Lotteries and gambling pretty much always lived on the periphery for me. It was never a major focus, but it always lingered around here and there.

Another watershed moment for me happened while dating a girl during my college years. A month or two into our relationship, I went to her house to meet her family. I knew their dad didn't live with them, but I didn't know much more than that. I do recall upon visiting, though, that the house felt disheveled and the people living in it seemed sad. And that was for good reason: her father had lost everything, including their prior house, on gambling at the horse track.

I've never been one to spend money on scratch tickets or Keno or anything like that. But I have always been fascinated with the obsession, the dream, and the constant conversations

I hear about the lottery and winning it. So many conversations start with "when I win the lottery." So I thought I'd write this book, not only to explore the lives of winners but also to help people understand the intricacies of what makes the lottery work operationally and what the true odds are. Unfortunately, your odds remain terrible.

That said, I had to put my money where my mouth is. While writing this book, I played the lottery far more than usual. Powerball, Mega Millions, and scratch tickets. Pretty often. The table on the following page shows the results and confirms my statement about the odds. Your money is best spent elsewhere if you're looking for a return on investment. If you're looking to have fun and you have some disposable income, more power to you. Enjoy.

Lastly, my father passed away in July 2023 during the copy-editing phase of this book process. He knew I finished it and was so immensely proud, but he will never be able to hold it in his hand and read it. I'm still struggling with that one, but I can say with utmost confidence that with the parent and person my father was, I hit the lottery.

I did it, Dad. *Finally.*

CHAPTER THIRTEEN
Lottery Log

During the course of writing this book, I decided to play various lottery games way more often than I typically do. I logged the results, and the next page will show how it all shook out. Spoiler: well, you probably know already.

Date	Game	Spend	Prize
11/7/2022	Powerball	$20	$4
12/28/2022	Mega Millions	$20	$0
1/2/2023	Mega Millions	$20	$0
1/5/2023	Mega Millions	$20	$0
1/8/2023	Mega Millions	$20	$4
12/6/2023	Scratch Tickets (2)	$40	$0
12/17/2023	Scratch Tickets (3)	$60	$0
1/20/2023	Mega Millions	$20	$0
1/26/2023	Powerball	$20	$0
2/4/2023	Powerball	$20	$4
2/6/2023	Powerball	$20	$0
2/10/2023	Mega Millions	$20	$0
2/11/2023	Scratch Ticket (1)	$10	$0
2/11/2023	Scratch Ticket (1)	$10	$0
2/11/2023	Mega Millions	$10	$4
2/13/2023	Powerball	$10	$0
2/17/2023	Scratch Ticket (1)	$10	$0
2/17/2023	Powerball	$20	$0
2/21/2023	Mega Millions	$20	$0
2/24/2023	Mega Millions	$20	$0
2/25/2023	Powerball	$20	$4
3/4/2023	Powerball	$20	$4
3/6/2023	Mega Millions	$12	$0
3/15/2023	Scratch Ticket (1)	$50	$100
3/15/2023	Scratch Ticket (1)	$10	$0
3/18/2023	Scratch Ticket (1)	$50	$0
3/18/2023	Scratch Ticket (1)	$50	$0
3/15/2023	Mega Millions	$10	$2
TOTAL	All Tickets	$632	$126

www.ingramcontent.com/pod-product-compliance
Lightning Source LLC
Chambersburg PA
CBHW050446150626
46551CB00029B/1796